THIS
IS
BIG

THIS
IS
BIG

HOW THE FOUNDER OF WEIGHT WATCHERS

CHANGED THE WORLD—AND ME

MARISA
MELTZER

Little, Brown and Company

New York Boston London

Little, Brown and Company
Hachette Book Group
1290 Avenue of the Americas, New York, NY 10104
littlebrown.com

First Edition: April 2020

Little, Brown and Company is a division of Hachette Book Group, Inc. The Little, Brown name and logo are trademarks of Hachette Book Group, Inc.

The publisher is not responsible for websites (or their content) that are not owned by the publisher.

The Hachette Speakers Bureau provides a wide range of authors for speaking events. To find out more, go to hachettespeakersbureau.com or call (866) 376-6591.

ISBN 978-0-316-41400-5
LCCN 2019945559

10 9 8 7 6 5 4 3 2 1

LSC-C

Printed in the United States of America

CONTENTS

Contents

AUTHOR'S NOTE

I wish that I had gotten a chance to meet Jean Nidetch. Her slim autobiography, *The Jean Nidetch Story,* was a starting point and an introduction to her inimitable voice. Luckily, Jean had been enough of a media star in her day that she'd left interviews, profiles, and television appearances to review and to quote from. I talked to people who knew Jean both personally and professionally, plus I spoke with historians, critics, and writers of her era and ours. I read issues of *Weight Watchers* magazine in sequence, spent days reading vintage cookbooks, made my way through archives, and bid on Jean-related memorabilia (including handwritten cards and a vinyl recording of her advice) on eBay. I found as much information as I could about her and drew my conclusions about her life from that research.

Some of Jean's many colorful anecdotes proved to be inaccurate or conflicting, whether because she was a fabulist or maybe because she just didn't have the best memory. For example, she told the story of the woman in the grocery store mistaking her for pregnant many times—sometimes it took place in September, sometimes October. In her autobiography, which she wrote in her mid-eighties, she recalled the Jessica Mitford article coming out in the early 1980s. I found it in Mitford's own archive; it was published in 1967. I never did find where she originally said, "It's choice, not chance, that determines your destiny." If I could verify a story from outside accounts, I did; otherwise I went with the version that seemed the most accurate from my research.

I was not reporting this book undercover. The company knew I was working on a book about Weight Watchers and cooperated with my research, as did group leaders and some members. But everyone deserves privacy—especially in the ups and downs of dieting—so I have changed several names, and some characters in the book are composites. A few passages have appeared previously in other publications, and timelines have been condensed or shifted.

PROLOGUE

It's choice, not chance, that determines
your destiny.

—Jean Nidetch

Jean Nidetch woke up one morning in September 1961 feeling sylphlike. "Did you know you could weigh two hundred and fourteen pounds and have a thin day?" she would later ask crowds who came to see her speak.

She put on a muumuu, a dress she considered a fat woman's boon because it hung nicely over everything and in the pockets she could squirrel away pistachios. The tag on the dress read size 10. In reality, Jean wore a size 44— roughly equivalent to a 20 in modern vanity sizing—but she'd had a seamstress remove the tags from her clothing and replace them with smaller, more cheering sizes. Her driver's license weight was 145 pounds, which she hadn't been since before high school. But nobody weighed you at the DMV.

Jean tied a ribbon in her hair. She walked through Little Neck to the supermarket, where she passed rows of Quisp cereal and stocked up on graham crackers for her young sons. She lingered in the sweets aisle, filling her cart with bright yellow boxes of the delicious, pillowy chocolate-covered marshmallow cookies called Mallomars. These were what she called her Frankenstein, a favorite treat and nemesis and the real reason she'd come to the store. She'd taken to hiding them in the hamper in her bathroom; she would sneak in, lock the door, and consume three satisfying boxes at a time. She tried to make a joke out of it: "One cookie plus one cookie equals eleven." Afterward, she always promised herself she'd quit Mallomars, but her resolve never lasted more than a few days.

That September morning Jean found herself back at the supermarket, stocking up once again. She would simply tell the checker the boxes of cookies were for her children. It was a cycle that she thought she'd never break. Being fat was just unlucky, and despite that, Jean felt like she had done well. She was thirty-eight years old, happily married to a nice husband who drove a bus and who was fatter than she was, which meant she could still feel small and ladylike. She had two healthy sons, ages five and ten. What more could Jean Nidetch of Queens, New York, in 1961 reasonably ask for?

Then Jean spotted a woman she'd met on occasion in the neighborhood, standing over by the cantaloupes. She hadn't especially liked her when they'd been introduced, but Jean was a good housewife and a purposely outgoing person. She figured that if she was going to be fat, at least she had to be friendly to make up for it.

"Jean, you look so wonderful," the woman told her. "Did you have a good summer?" Jean, flattered, answered that she had. She thought not of sun and sand but of the concession trucks that made their way along the streets of Little Neck selling ice cream, doughnuts, pizza, and sandwiches, trucks that she'd run to catch up to, something only kids were supposed to do.

"You look so marvelous," the woman said again, looking her up and down. "When are you due?"

To say that it was a moment that she would never forget is an understatement; it would define and transform the rest of her life. But at the time, Jean, the ultimate chatterbox, was dumbstruck. That woman thought she was pregnant. Eventually, Jean stammered something about how she had to go and made her way home in a hasty retreat.

"What do I do now?" she kept asking herself as she walked the four blocks home. Once she made it back, she stood in front of the full-length mirror behind her bedroom door. It was something she normally tried to avoid. Jean was fine with her reflection in the bathroom mirror—the face, the lipstick, and the hair she could get just right. She'd walk away thinking her eyes were gorgeous. This time, though, she looked hard at her hips and stomach. Bulges. Who was she to be having a thin day?

Later Jean would write, "Most fat people need to be hurt in some way in order to be jolted into taking action and doing something for themselves. Something has got to happen to demoralize you suddenly and completely before you see the light."

She decided right there in front of the full-length mirror to be grateful to the woman at the supermarket, not because she liked her or would forgive her, but because she'd given Jean what she needed.

THIS
IS
BIG

INTRODUCTION

*J*ean Nidetch is dead.

I have the slightly morbid habit of reading the *New York Times* obituary section every morning, usually while sitting at the wooden kitchen table in my Brooklyn apartment, drinking coffee while my bulldog, Joan, snores at my feet, exhausted from her twenty minutes of walking. An obituary takes someone's life and compresses it into a neat arc of beginnings, highlights, lowlights, and endings, which is why I enjoy reading them before I go off and make my way through my own work as a writer as well as my life, in both of which I often feel like I'm traveling from one slippery point to an unknown other, lacking coherence or a plan. In obituaries, I have a subconscious wish to see in one illuminating flash how another person figured out her story so I can gain some insight into mine. It was mostly a soothing habit, until the morning I read about Jean.

In late April 2015 the obit headline read, "Jean Nidetch, a Founder of Weight Watchers, Dies at 91." I must have looked confused—it had not ever occurred to me that an actual person had thought up Weight Watchers. To me, at thirty-eight years old, the ubiquitous weight-loss company had no origin story; it had always just existed.

Existed, I thought, to torment me. *Tortured* would be a polite way to label my relationship to dieting, which I had pursued my whole life. I can't even recall how old I was when my parents put me on my first diet. Four? Five? I think I was nine when they signed me up for Weight Watchers. That was what passed for smart parenting in the 1980s. Weight Watchers didn't last more than a few weeks. And it didn't work. None of the diets ever did. They still don't. I am a chronic, classic yo-yo dieter whose weight has risen and fallen so many times that, if charted, it would resemble a city skyline.

But there was Jean Nidetch smiling at me from the home page of the *New York Times,* with big owl-like glasses and a blond bouffant, holding a piece of cake she clearly had no intention of eating. My first thought was that finally I had a face to put to my misery. Was this the she-devil who'd started it all, the one who made weight loss seem like a fait accompli if only you cared enough about it? I read Jean's obituary, eager to give myself a target to blame for my own Sisyphean attempts at dieting and all the attendant obsession and frustration. I thought I knew just what the story of her life would be, some variation of a thin woman becomes rich and famous butting into overweight people's lives, never giving them a moment's respite from calorie-counting or branded no-fat frozen treats.

But as I read, I didn't see a villain in Jean Nidetch; I saw myself. Here was a woman who also had spent a lifetime thinking about her weight. Jean had been a chubby kid who turned into a fat adult, a woman who wrestled with a raging sweet tooth and whose preferred method of consumption was not enjoying a slice of fancy cake with friends but rather inhaling an entire package of her favorite supermarket cookies in the privacy of her own bathroom. Jean and I were both five foot seven, Jewish, blond (hers by bottle, mine by birth), and residents of Brooklyn (hers by birth, mine by adoption). When I look at old photos of her before she lost the weight, the physical resemblance between us is so strong, she could easily be my aunt or cousin; she could almost be me somehow transported back in time to New York City in 1961.

I realized that I was the same age as Jean was when she'd begun to lose the weight and transform her life beyond her own—and anyone else's—wildest expectations. Her rock-bottom moment was when someone mistakenly assumed she was pregnant. Dozens of people have mistakenly assumed I was pregnant—at the airport, on the subway, at restaurants as I sat next to my own thin mother. One woman at the department store Barneys wouldn't even take no for an answer. "You must be at least postpartum," she said and stared at my abdomen. I blushed, shook my head, and tried to look busy browsing scarves. I made a mental note never to wear the gray hoodie I had on again.

Jean also sounded so human, a woman who'd struggled with love and age and work and family and her place in the world. So instead of delighting in the demise of a newfound nemesis, by the time I finished reading the abbreviated version of Jean Nidetch's life, I felt a moment of connection between us.

My job as a journalist who writes a lot about the world of beauty and wellness and fitness entails sampling treatments and sometimes spending time with famous people. It's a life that I've worked hard for and I love being part of the glittery landscape of New York. I also feel like I live in a world of thin people. I know their habits but I'm also aware that I am not one of them. The irony that I professionally subject my body to the advice of others is not lost on me. I know that part of what makes me good at writing about these procedures is the fact that I am not a swanlike woman with an absence of cellulite and the gift of natural athletic ability. What I don't get to share publicly is my occasional ambivalence, that sometimes I feel low talking to gurus who promise that their rainbow-based diet will solve my weight problems or trainers who tell me they're just dying to get me on a cardio program.

I have never had a healthy relationship with food. Given the tender age at which I started dieting, I probably never had the chance to form one.

Once, I went to a photo shoot to meet the actress Emily Blunt for a British *Vogue* cover story I was writing. She was getting her hair and makeup done, so I was killing time before we were introduced, wandering around the location, a massive nineteenth-century industrial building in Long Island City that had been turned into a lush venue teeming with ivy on its brick walls that you could rent for weddings and the like. I set my bag on a green velvet sofa and eventually made my way to a table strewn with the remnants of a catered lunch: quinoa salad, grilled chicken, iced tea, and a plate of dairy-free, flourless brownies sitting next to a bouquet of flowers. I sat down and ate one brownie after another, the way I always eat things—the way Jean probably once ate things—without savoring them, as if the act of eating needed to be gotten over with as quickly as possible. With no dairy or flour, the brownies were almost healthy, I figured. A bearded photography assistant wandered inside to get a cable while I was stuffing my face. I turned my back to him, as if that would hide my crime of appetite.

The shoot was just a few weeks after Blunt had given birth to her second daughter—"my Bean," she called her in her lilting accent—and I'm so nosy that I'd snuck first thing into the wardrobe area of the shoot to see what size jeans she currently wore: 26. Which is about a size 2.

Emily Blunt finally came down the stairs from hair and makeup, trailed by a baby nurse carrying a tiny infant. Blunt smiled graciously and gestured toward the brownies. "You really must try one," she said to me and the nurse, adding that the brownies were just so good, so rich, that she was satisfied with *just* one small bite and in fact could not *possibly* eat more; that's how rich they were. Was this how normal people's brains reacted to food—one nibble and you were satisfied? I had eaten perhaps four brownies in the span of less than five minutes and stuffed another half a dozen in my bag to devour at home, alone. (I'd also taken a few sad-looking pieces of cold chicken for the dog.) When I'd heard Blunt coming down the stairs, there was just enough time to re-arrange the remaining brownies on the plate so it didn't look like a troop of ravenous Girl Scouts had been at them. I was privately embarrassed by my behavior and jealous of Blunt at the same time. Maybe that's how you maintain a size 26, even postpartum, only eating one small bite of one brownie when confronted with a plate of them. I know now what Jean would say: "Not eating the hot fudge sundae has to be more important than eating the largest, richest hot fudge sundae in the world."

For the past several years I have felt trapped between dieting my way to a slimmer body and simply giving up and trying to love myself as is, caught between change and acceptance. But no matter how unattainable perfection may be, working toward it—as opposed to working toward self-acceptance—is satisfying in its own way. There's action involved in inching closer to a goal, even one you can't attain—counting calories, working out, weighing in. At least you're aiming for something tangible. I would like to feel better in my body. I would like to be able to climb subway stairs fast without feeling out of breath; I would like to be able to see a picture of myself and not have it ruin my day; I would like to have a much less emotional relationship with food. But at the same time, am I a fool for still, after all these yo-yo years, wanting to lose and keep off weight when I know that, statistically, it's rare?

Jean Nidetch was a woman who succeeded where I— and millions—had failed. She lost seventy-plus pounds and kept them off, then she founded a company and became a mogul, and all of this was over fifty years ago, when help-wanted ads were still divided by gender. She basically earned the American dream. On that same spring day I read Jean's obituary, I took out my journal—I've kept one since I was a teenager—and wrote down a list of questions I wished I could ask her, questions whose answers might help me with my own life. How had she succeeded while others struggled? What made her so different from other housewives? What did it really take to change—effort or luck or the support of people around her? Sheer determination? What did it feel like to transform?

In the days and weeks after I read that obituary, I couldn't stop thinking about Jean. Jean wasn't there to answer my questions, of course, and the internet yielded surprisingly little about a woman who had accomplished so much. I began to wonder if I could find the answers another way. I'm a journalist. So what if an assignment editor wasn't pushing me to write about Jean? What if I assigned Jean to myself?

Jean's life and mine were very different. I'm not a frustrated housewife with two young sons. Rather, I'm the kind of person who makes watercolors of sunsets in the summer while drinking cocktails on my roof, who reads a book a week and goes to French movies. My friends often cite my life as being an inspiration to them, and I have quite rigorously assembled something that looks really good from the outside. But that performance has always been a stark contrast to how I feel about myself. I had a gut feeling that Jean Nidetch knew all about that soul-killing mismatch.

I've never been afraid to go all in for my assignments. I've been to all-women camps where a group would chant "Man on land" just to let you know men had come to clean the outhouses; I've had a shaman tell me I was a lake in a former life (and then tell me a spirit told him I should lose weight); I've let near strangers lead me off-trail hiking through the redwoods. I am brave, and I am dedicated, and I decided I was going to join Weight Watchers for real. With a good attitude. I admit I had long dismissed Weight Watchers as the most retro, basic, lowest-common-denominator, least chic diet company in the world. But it worked for Jean, and if I wanted to find a way out of this constant struggle and understand a woman who conquered weight for herself and others, why not? I was constantly on a diet, so why not *that* diet? Plus I hadn't ever been on one single diet for a whole year before. I didn't think I would lose seventy pounds like Jean did, although I had before, and gained it all back and then some. If I lost a pound a week, I would be fifty pounds lighter in a year, but what else could happen? Every diet is a promise that if you change your weight, you'll change your life. What did transformation mean to me after all these years of chasing one?

So maybe this time would be different. No goal weights, for one. I wanted the year ahead to be about strength and triumph, but I wasn't naive and I knew I couldn't predict how it would go. It was about losing some weight, not the impossible quest of eliminating every last cosmetically unappealing ounce. Rather than fixating on numbers on a scale, I was interested in coming to terms with myself and trying to break some of my worst lifelong habits. I knew there was room to learn, and to change, and to find some peace.

CHAPTER ONE

I WAS EVEN A FAT CHILD

1923

Jean Nidetch didn't consider the term *fat* to be a dirty word; it was more a statement of fact. "I was even a fat child—I haven't forgotten it," she was fond of saying, her strong Outer Borough accent turning *child* into "chi-auld." "I wanted to be the pretty one. A fat kid never hears the words *pretty, adorable, cute, handsome*. Instead they're always *good, honest, neat, clean, trustworthy*." She spent her childhood in Brooklyn feeling various kinds of shame for the way she looked. She was too embarrassed to climb on top of the merry-go-round; in school classrooms, she had recurring anxiety that made her sit on the edge of her seat, nervous about an impending fire drill. "I'm always the last one to hoist out of my seat and get out of the room and surely I would knock over the books or the ink or another kid."

She was born Jean Evelyn Slutsky—named after the actress Jeanne Eagels—in Brooklyn on October 12, 1923. Her father,

David Slutsky, was a cabdriver; he was naturally thin, the kind of person who would forget to eat. Her mother, Mae Rodin Slutsky, was a manicurist, and she had the same zaftig body that her daughters, Jean and her younger sister, Helen, inherited. Jean grew up in a working-class, Jewish, Depression-era household in a pre-gentrified Brooklyn; her grandfather had immigrated to the United States from Russia and sold pickles and herring out of a pushcart in Williamsburg long before that neighborhood was populated with boutique hotels and a Whole Foods.

At night Jean's mother would make dinner and eat with the girls while their father was working a late shift, then she'd sit down and have a second dinner with him once he got home. Food was both a reward and a comfort, her family's antidote to sorrow and its way to celebrate good news—steak and french fries for Sunday dinners, penny candy by the handful, egg creams made with U-Bet chocolate syrup and nonhomogenized milk from Borden with Elsie the Cow on the bottle and cream on the top. Food was a balm for sadness too. If Jean cried, her family would give her something to eat. Her father took a certain pride in having a fat wife and daughters during the Depression, a sign that he was a good breadwinner able to keep the cupboards from going bare.

Still, Jean was bubbly, extroverted, and talkative. She grew up in an age when Dale Carnegie's *How to Win Friends and Influence People* and Marjorie Hillis's *Live Alone and Like It: A Guide for the Extra Woman*, both out in 1936, were bestsellers, self-help books propounding ideas of positive thinking, self-reliance, and reinvention, three concepts she would embody over the course of her life. Jean preferred to date boys who were overweight and she avoided the thin girls—she wanted to be the thinnest one in any given group. She claimed that finding clothes that fit was a constant challenge and she started experimenting with fad diets before high school. "Jeanne" (which was either a misspelling of her name or some kind of youthful dalliance with a more European spelling) Slutsky went to Girls High School, an all-girls public school located on Nostrand Avenue in Brooklyn, and was the vice president of her senior class; she graduated in 1941. In her yearbook photo, she had a round face and the same gently curled hairstyle that had seemingly swept the entire senior class that year, but you wouldn't consider her more than maybe a little chubby. Her senior quote was from Ralph Waldo Emerson's essay "Considerations by the Way": "A day for toil, an hour for sport / But for a friend is life too short."

Being thin wasn't a preoccupation of Jean's alone; in that same yearbook, a fellow student named Germaine wrote an essay titled "This Too, Too Solid Flesh"—a quote from *Hamlet*—that began in dramatic teenage fashion: "Nobody loves a fat girl, and who knows better than I the sorrows of the flesh?" Germaine described various diets she'd attempted—the two-week milk diet, four-day orange juice diet—and wrote about going to an endocrine clinic, where she submitted to a strict diet of its prescription. After two weeks, she gained a few pounds and resolved to stop dieting. Not that this was necessarily a proto–body acceptance work. In the end Germaine concluded, "Now I am six pounds heavier than I have ever been before, and I am firmly convinced that as years go by, my feet will sink more deeply into the sod beneath them. Indeed my footprints will be left on the sands of time."

Jean's obsession with her body reflected the relatively new phenomenon of blue-collar families trying to lose weight, once the pursuit of the wealthy. By the World War II era Jean graduated into, being fat was deeply entrenched in American culture as bad—undesirable, lazy, and inviting mockery. Jean dreaded that fate for herself.

The urge to diet doesn't come solely from vanity, or family, or habit, or the desire for better health, or society. The best summation I have found is in Hillel Schwartz's book *Never Satisfied*, a history of dieting in America.

> The desire to be slim is not simply a result of fashion. It must be understood in terms of a confluence of movements in the sciences and in dance, in home economics and political economy, in medical technology and food marketing, in evangelical religion and life insurance. Our sense of the body, of its heft and momentum, is shaped more by the theater of our lives than by our costume. Our furniture, our toys, our architecture, our etiquette are designed for, or impel us toward, a certain kind of body and a certain feeling of weight.

What is considered fat and thin is constantly constructed and updated, subject to the whims of society as much as anything else. While dieting sits at the center of so many seemingly unrelated movements and ideas, the fact is that it places a human being in the middle of these conflicts. Dieting holds out the promise that much can be solved by changing a single person.

Dieting—the word comes from the ancient Greek word *diaita,* meaning "a way of life"—had for centuries been the preoccupation and the luxury of those with disposable incomes. Being fat was tied to excess. Benjamin Franklin wrote, "Eat for necessity, not pleasure, for lust knows not where necessity ends." And for a long time, dieting was the province of men, who were trying to fight off the extra pounds put on by industrialization. When you go from working on farms or doing other kinds of physical labor to joining the professional classes, you have to either adjust what you eat or get used to some extra weight. Words like *porky, butterball, jumbo,* and *slob* came into the vernacular in the second half of the nineteenth century to describe overweight men.

The middle-class battle against fatness began in the United States around the late nineteenth century. Then, as now, there were fad diets driven by personalities, one of whom was William Banting. Born in 1796, the obese British undertaker followed the advice of his physician, Dr. William Harvey, to limit carbohydrates, and he lost weight. In 1863, he published his plan in a pamphlet, offering it as an alternative to curbing the appetite with cocaine, and the Harvey-Banting diet was born. It mainly prohibited sweets and starches, among them bread, beer, potatoes, and sugar, as well as butter and milk. His name was so well known it became a verb synonymous with dieting; people asked each other, "Are you Banting?"

At the Battle Creek Sanitarium in Michigan, former broom salesman John H. Kellogg based his eating plan on the vegetarian Seventh-Day Adventist diet, which didn't allow meat, alcohol, caffeine, leavened bread, or condiments. The sensuous nature of food was considered, well, sensual—

gastrointestinal problems were linked to sex. John's brother and bookkeeper W. K. Kellogg started the Battle Creek Toasted Corn Flake Company, which later became the Kellogg Company, of cereal fame. (Another nineteenth-century health advocate, the minister Sylvester Graham, preached the gospel of whole-grain bread and was the namesake for the graham cracker.) Horace Fletcher, aka "the Great Masticator," led the chewing craze, the adherents of which chewed each mouthful of food one hundred times before swallowing it. The movement had such high-profile followers as Henry Ford, John D. Rockefeller, Thomas Edison, and Upton Sinclair.

Gradually, in the years from 1880 to 1920, there was a shift in cultural norms; if you were fat, you were not just undesirable; you were physically and morally bad, and that went for women as well as men. While being called plump was once considered a compliment for a woman, meaning she was robust and of optimal health for childbearing (a woman's primary goal), that ideal changed. The new paragon was personified by the Gibson Girls in the pen-and-ink drawings of Charles Dana Gibson, idealized women with slender, hourglass figures. Being fat became about abundance of appetite, of wanting too much and being lazy on top of that. By 1898, the *Ladies' Home Journal* (which in 1903 became the first magazine to hit a million subscribers) began a monthly series of domestic lessons written by one Mrs. S. T. Rorer that covered topics like indigestion and avoiding overeating rich foods. In 1910, the *Chicago Daily Tribune* asked, "Are society women literally killing themselves to keep thin?" In 1911, *Good Housekeeping* published a satirical essay by Maria Middlebury (possibly a pseudonym, given that the byline never again appeared in their archive of writers, which included Edna St. Vincent Millay and Virginia Woolf) called "My Week Without Food." It began with a flourish: "Having been always a more than average healthy person, I found myself in middle age confronted with gouty conditions that culminated in arthritis in the finger joints, a disease which slowly but surely disables the hands." This condition was incurable, her family doctor said. "From that moment dated my fall from the ranks of common-sense, normal women, to the army of cranks and faddists...I chanced upon some articles about fasting, and thought they pointed out a possible road to salvation." The first day she had a tablespoon of coffee to prevent a headache; it didn't work. The second day she stared into space and thought of nothing but food. After a brief respite of feeling "light and supple," she felt like she was getting the flu. Apart from drinking some juice, she stuck to her no-food diet. Her weight went from 170 to 154. At the end, she wrote, "I printed out a neat little card reading: *Yes, I've stopped now. No, not very bad. Sixteen pounds. Yes, I know I look ten years older, but I shall be younger in a week. No, I'm not eating more than usual now, etc.*"

World War I was another turning point. The American government's propaganda posters from the era encouraged consumers to buy food with thought and serve just enough; some exhorted civilians to observe a meatless day and wheatless days to help conserve food for the troops. Weight was quickly becoming a national concern. Bathroom scales had arrived in American homes soon after the First World War, and the maintenance of weight could now become a constant, at-home surveillance. The concept of the calorie was popularized by the doctor and health columnist Lulu Hunt Peters, whose book *Diet and Health with Key to the Calories* was a bestseller in 1918. Peters wrote of how she had lost over fifty pounds by counting calories and assured her readers that she knew firsthand the pain of being fat and the glory that awaited them if they could learn to resist temptation.

By the 1920s, the nascent women's movement had successfully organized for political gain—most notably the right to vote—which increased women's public presence. Beauty was about a lot more than the female face; now the female body was shown off in a new way: girls bobbed their hair, clothes were tighter, and skirts were shorter. Flappers with their appetite-killing cigarettes were the height of chic. Due to its restriction of mobility and the fear that it might cause organ damage, the corset was phased out of fashion, leaving women to contend with the natural shape of their bodies once more. At the same time, women started to buy store-bought clothing rather than having dresses made or making dresses themselves, and with ready-to-wear came sizes and clothes women had to fit into rather than be fitted for (it also brought up the issues that come with comparing one's own size to someone else's). Among college girls in the 1920s, a lamb-chop-and-pineapple diet was hugely popular. Slimming down was undertaken at least partly to emulate the thin actors starring in motion pictures, including Mary Pickford and Theda Bara. The advent of widespread photography in magazines made images of famous women—and the unattainable and enhanced ideal they represented—more readily accessible.

During the Great Depression, Americans struggling to

support themselves ate less meat and more sugar out of financial necessity, and meals could be stretched with gravy or bread or potatoes. Margarine was considered a light alternative to butter. Processed foods began to appear in the kitchens as a convenience and a money-saver. Velveeta and Rice Krispies were both introduced in 1928; the canned meat Spam, Skippy peanut butter, and Ritz crackers (which formed the basis of a popular mock-apple pie) came on the market in the 1930s.

World War II, symbolized by the "We can do it" arm-flexing icon of Rosie the Riveter, gave women a momentary position of power outside the home, aiding the workforce. But when that was over, it was time for the girls at home to get in shape. In 1932 Benzedrine was developed for the relief of asthma, but the amphetamine would become widely used in later decades as a diet pill and diet secret at a time when women's magazines counseled against second helpings. Magazines published quick thousand-calorie-per-day plans. In her syndicated nutrition column, the writer Ida Jean Kain (who would later coin the phrase "The way to a man's heart is through his stomach") wrote, "Six million GIs will soon be home, you know! Competition is rugged. For the first time in history there won't be enough men to go around."

Jean met her future first husband after he left the army in 1945. Before that, she had won a partial scholarship to Long Island University but couldn't pay the rest of the tuition. "None of the Rosies I knew had become riveters," she said, making the point that higher education hadn't been emphasized much in her peer group even though she had excelled at math in high school and had parents who prized education. She compromised, attending the City College of New York, which was free, and studying business administration. She was there for a year but left when her father, a lifelong heavy smoker, died of pneumonia in 1942. She had to get a job to help support her family. Her mother thought her daughter should follow in her own footsteps and become a manicurist, that there was power in holding another woman's hand as she talked about her life. Jean countered that she couldn't even file her own nails. She ended up attending night school and went to work for a furniture company in Queens. Then she was offered a job closer to home at a company called Man o' War Publishing, which produced a tip sheet for horse races and whose employees took bets in the back rooms of their own publishing house. If there was any indication the business might not have been completely legal, Jean denied understanding it at the time. Gambling would prove to be one of Jean's enduring passions; it gave her the same easy pleasure and rush of highly caloric foods and was something she would indulge in long after she gave up cookies. When policemen came to close the business pending an investigation, she knew it was time to find another job. The safest and most legal place she could think of was the Internal Revenue Service, which happened to be hiring clerks.

The best part of that job was the coffee breaks. Jean would get a Danish or a piece of cake at a luncheonette across the street and chat with whoever was around. The restaurant's owner introduced her to Marty Nidetch, who, at 265 pounds, was larger than her. They sat next to each other, both eating, and started talking. He was good-looking and had a healthy sense of humor. "Hi, I'm Jean," she said. "That looks good," Marty replied. Was he talking about her pastries or the way she looked? Women were supposed to be light eaters, but Jean was not. Their love was a tale of two gourmands. "Marty and I fell in love and we loved to eat. Marty knew every restaurant in New York that did second helpings, and we knew every restaurant in Queens that didn't charge for dessert."

CHAPTER TWO

IS THERE
A TYPICAL FAT GIRL?

July 2017

What's your why? is a popular question at Weight Watchers. There are hats emblazoned with it that you could in theory wear, but frankly, I would rather get a sunburn. I hate being asked why I'm trying to lose weight. Isn't dieting one thing that you don't have to justify? Can't you see my stomach grazing the table when I slide into booths and that I can't really cross my legs? You see an unflattering photo or your pants don't fit, and the jig is up.

"I'm joining Weight Watchers," I told my friend Vera while we were sitting together in a steam room at a bathhouse. "I don't want to die and leave specific instructions in my will to dress me in a long-sleeved top because I hate my arms." Vera is my idealized version of what a cool woman is. Fifteen years ago, we were both low-ranking employees at a magazine, though she had been there a year longer than I had and knew the ropes and, crucially, how to deal with the terrible editor in chief who routinely yelled at me about typos while chomping nicotine gum. At some point I stopped going to a closet or a bathroom stall to cry and just sobbed into my hands at my desk. After six months at the magazine I was laid off, and Vera took me out to celebrate with margaritas followed by a then-novel Brazilian wax, my first. She became my confidante and has remained so ever since.

We talked about bodies all the time but in a heady way that was removed from ourselves. We also talked about beauty standards but not the reality of how we felt they applied to us. I knew she'd struggled with an eating disorder from high school through her mid-twenties—I guess you never stop struggling—but she was tall and lithe, the kind of person who actually looked good in dramatically flared pants. Even during women's hours at the bathhouse, she was wearing a black string bikini; she'd had two kids, but she was thin and had a taut enough stomach that it remained flat when she sat. My stomach, on the other hand, was barely contained in a high-waisted bikini bottom. I was nearly constantly aware of the feeling of my stomach hanging down toward my pelvis, of my thighs rubbing together, of the fat under my chin touching my neck when I looked down. And I had tried my best to change my body. I'd done all of it—dieting, working out, spas, personal trainers, radical body acceptance, Botox, fillers, Kybella in an attempt to get rid of a double chin. I'd even gone under general anesthesia for liposuction. And that list is not complete.

After I made my Weight Watchers announcement, I could tell Vera was doing some kind of quick calculation in her head, trying to respond supportively without offending me.

Vera tells me I'm hot all the time, in the casual way that female friends level each other with a barrage of compliments. I believe her when she says that, but I also suspect that if she were my size, she would hate herself. She's probably my closest friend but she still thinks that I was having a cyst removed when I was actually having liposuction—that was the lie I told everyone. That's the kind of insecurity that, as close as we are, goes unspoken. "But you're so bodacious," she finally said. I tried not to roll my eyes. I was fat, at least by the standards of coastal America, where I had spent my whole life. I say *fat* not as a reclamation but as a no-frills description. I hate every euphemism—*curvy, plus-size,* whatever. I dated a guy who said I was "carrying extra weight," and I somehow convinced myself that was sweet.

At my heaviest, like right then, I wore a size 16, which I know is not actually that fat. My body was tragic but also ordinary. Or maybe fat has just become normal. According to the Centers for Disease Control, in the United States, over two-thirds of adults and 31.8 percent of children and adolescents are overweight or obese. And most of them are trying hard to get thinner; roughly forty-five million Americans diet each year, and they spend some $33 billion on weight-loss products.

Is there a typical fat girl? Probably not, but I certainly never fit the mousy type found in young-adult novels. I've always genuinely enjoyed swimsuit shopping; I eat healthy food, and I exercise regularly. I'm confident in my professional abilities and my right to be present where I choose to be. I have no fear of public speaking or expressing my opinions, and I have the assurance of someone who has been told many times that she's intelligent and talented. No one would ever mistake me for a wallflower. I've loved clothes all my life and I know I have good taste and an eye for how to dress. I was raised by parents who told me to wear whatever pleased me in the moment. That advice translated into some very colorful outfits in childhood photos (I had a red shirt with a traditional Japanese print of a fish on it that I wore daily for all of first grade), but "wear whatever you please" also became a kind of personal mantra. Clothing really can be armor.

I have days, or sometimes just hours, when I feel adequate, like someone could and should desire me for what I look like. But most of the time, I want to change it all. The ideal me (someone who can wear a size 6, who doesn't get rashes from her thighs brushing together as she walks, who has sculpted arms and a single chin) is a distant, shimmering spot on the horizon I'll never reach. But loving my own body just as it is feels equally elusive. Sometimes it's easier to describe my feelings about my body in terms of how I *don't* feel: I don't feel worthless. I don't feel trapped in it, necessarily. I'm good at yoga, which is not a very yogic thing to say, but I like how it makes my body feel wrung out and limber. I'm one of the best riders in my SoulCycle class and I can get through a Barry's Bootcamp class, although just barely, and I have to nap for two hours afterward. And yet I know yoga would be easier with less belly fat getting in the way of my forward folds and that I wouldn't be one of the slowest runners at boot camp if I were leaner. In some ways, I'm a fat stereotype. I love eating furtively, or at least I love how soothed I feel while I do it. I blame everything that doesn't go well in my life, like dating, on my weight.

I've tried for years to wear my heaviness with a certain hard-won pride. I flirted with fat acceptance, tried to believe that weight should not define a person and that beauty comes in different packages. But was that even possible if you weren't living alone without Wi-Fi in a yurt in Montana? I want my body to look good to *me* first and to the rest of the world second. I want to be someone whom I'd aspire to be if I were another woman or whom I would desire if I were a man. But I also want to reach some level of acceptance of the body I have, regardless of my weight.

I cannot remember the first person who called me fat. Nor can I remember the moment when it dawned on me that my body was fat and that fat was undesirable. I don't know how I got fat. I have always been fat; it's the only reality I can remember. Many people who write about their bodies speak of a time, usually a rose-tinted moment before puberty, when they took simple pleasure in their bodies, an era before the harsh realities of the outside world forced their way in. I never had that before-the-fall moment. There was no Joni Mitchell–style "We've got to get ourselves back to the garden" for my body. And perhaps because of this, I am suspicious of proclaimed Edens and even more suspicious of people who long for simpler times as a way of getting there.

My parents are both the kind of people who live in California—where I grew up, and where they did too—because they love being outside. My mother's favorite colors to wear are green and brown because they remind her of nature and of Robin Hood (she is a socialist). When I was growing up, my mother cherished her annual hiking trip with her girlfriends—they called themselves the 'Biner Sisters, from *carabiner*—to remote parts of the Sierras where they made jokes about bears and menstruation. I was disgusted by this as a seven-year-old and couldn't wait until I could trade in the college town where I grew up for a place with better department stores. I spent many weekends being dragged on various trails all over the West Coast, lured with promises that I could order whatever I wanted when we went out to eat, even dessert. Still, I complained the entire time about how tired and bored I was.

This was California in the 1980s—redwood hot tubs, glass bricks, grilled swordfish I requested for my birthday meal. We shopped for organic produce and drank fresh-squeezed juices and green smoothies decades before that was considered chic. My mother frequented Jazzercise classes; my father had started surfing as a teenager. Vacations were spent swimming and mountain biking in Yosemite; winters were for skiing in British Columbia or Colorado. My hair was white-blond, bleached from the sun.

My parents split when I was a toddler. I have only vague early memories of them in the same room together and they involve hearing them argue or watching my father eating steak dipped in vinaigrette salad dressing that my mother prepared. Not that she ate it. Her thing, her diet trick, I guess, is that she doesn't eat dinner, ever. She grew up in Silicon Valley before it was called that, the daughter of a Southern woman whose signature Jell-O dish was a concoction of Coca-Cola, green olives, and nuts. My mom always seemed to resent cooking, but it was bigger than that; she resented food. Not that she has ever been fat—she is the sort who is perennially trying to lose ten pounds so she can fit into a size

4. Some of my earliest memories are watching her leave for her daily five-mile jog with our pet Siberian husky. This was the same woman who worked for Planned Parenthood, who took me to protests against the Miss California pageant and to lectures by Gloria Steinem. She told me recently that, in her mid-sixties, she "went wild with the beat" dancing at a Pussy Riot concert. My father is a gourmand who has made regular, albeit halfhearted, attempts to lose twenty pounds for the past thirty years but who never had real problems with weight. He invents his own diets with rules that don't adhere to science or sense. Like, he can't eat bread, but he can eat crackers. Sugar might be out, but a triple cappuccino made with half-and-half is fine. A few years ago his beloved border collie, Finn, needed to lose a few pounds, and his big idea was to go on a diet at the same time as his dog and chronicle it in a book he would call *The Dog Diet*. We agreed it had bestseller potential. He is a trial lawyer whose depictions in courtroom sketches seem to haunt him. More than once he has shown me a drawing of himself in a suit gesturing to make a point and asked me if I thought he looked fat. The only appropriate answer is no.

I don't recall having a lot of sit-down, well-balanced family meals. I'm not sure I ever got the opportunity to learn proper eating habits. I'm an only child and my parents were far from amicably separated, but they could easily focus on and communicate about my weight. Their main fear was that I would have to start buying clothes from a special section. They took me to my first dietitian when I was a toddler. I can't remember what was prescribed or how much I weighed or how old I was exactly. Even though I imagine their intentions were pure enough, what stays with me is the sense that I was being singled out and punished for reasons I couldn't understand. Dieting was really the only source of discipline in my life, partly because neither one of my parents was particularly strict, and partly because they didn't need to be—I was an exceedingly good little kid whose fantasy life mostly involved eating scones at tea parties.

My first round of Weight Watchers followed a few years later, when I was still in elementary school. My mother and I joined together—parent-and-child dieting was more acceptable in the mid-1980s—getting weighed in once a week in a strip mall in Northern California. I remember the night before the diet was to begin, I went to the refrigerator for some Newman's Own lemonade, and my mother told me, "That's your last glass. You don't want to drink your calories." Now, over thirty years later, the idea of not wasting calories on beverages still haunts me every time I drink grapefruit juice or order a margarita.

The standard routine as imposed by my parents was that when we entered a restaurant, one of them would tell me what I was allowed to eat—shish kebab or salad, for example, but never bagels or fried chicken or egg rolls on a stick sold by a local bodega. To this day they will comment on what I order. "A carne asada burrito? Well, at least you didn't get chips," my mother observed the last time I visited her, fixing me with a meaningful stare that really dialed down my enjoyment of said burrito. "Do me a favor and eat slowly," my dad said over dinner recently. Sometimes as a kid, I would beg enough or they'd be busy enough that they'd break down and let me eat what I wanted—a taquito or a slice of pizza or a brownie or a scoop of chocolate malted crunch ice cream from Thrifty—then immediately tell me that I was going to gain weight.

My unruly body was a family concern that everyone was invited to discuss. None of my mother's friends had a problem taking me aside at a party to talk to me about how I needed to watch my weight or to comment on whether I looked thinner that day. My body, the food I wanted to eat—none of it was my own, and that is how it became the defining relationship of my life.

In photos from the time, I'm only mildly chubby, but my family wanted me to be happy and healthy and to shield me from the ridicule of others. It didn't work. I remember being at a small grocery store with my mom, a place called, perhaps ironically, Piggy's Market, and hearing an older man in the checkout line say to her, "Why are you so thin and your daughter is so fat?" I'm not making this up. What kind of grown-up is that mean for no reason? And just what did he expect her to say? I remember her looking uncomfortable and saying, "I don't know." Perhaps she was too shocked to say anything else, but what I heard was her lack of loyalty. My parents wanted me to get a handle on my weight not just to save me from pain but to spare themselves the embarrassment of having a fat child.

I was a precocious girl, an indoor kid who just wanted to be left alone to read. (*Jane Eyre*, the Baby-Sitters Club series, Judy Blume's *Blubber*, Nancy Drew, or rather her plump friend Bess Marvin, a kind of comic foil who was boy-crazy and always failing at dieting.) School was effortless for me, but succeeding at food and my body, not so much. I thought

I hated all kinds of fitness, sports, and exercise because I was bad at them—so bad that I had to go to adaptive PE in elementary school, PE modified for those with disabilities. I was never clear on what my disability was, but I knew that my body could never be exceptional. I spent several summers at a hellish boot camp–like Junior Lifeguarding program where one particularly sadistic fellow eight-year-old camper nicknamed me Chubs when he saw me in my regulation red swimsuit. I don't think my parents realized how unhappy I was, perhaps because I didn't know how to communicate it to them. I did know there was another world out there, one with chocolate-dipped Kudos snack bars and families who ate well-balanced meals together. That wasn't my life. To this day, to me, the most foreign part of European movies is how they'll eat two bites of dessert or have fruit as a snack.

But what began as something that was forced on me— losing weight—slowly became something I wanted for myself. I dieted not just because my parents had instilled it in me as a kind of religion but because I wanted to look good too. Their desire to shelter me from the pain of being teased or singled out for being different—the best of intentions— worked, but they failed at teaching me any kind of healthy habits or even how to love myself. Having unrealistic goals for weight loss made maintaining healthy habits even more difficult.

A change happened around the age of ten, when, while flipping through the back pages of *Sunset* magazine, I saw a weight-loss camp for girls. A few weeks later I was an unaccompanied minor flying to Santa Barbara for two weeks of fat camp. My bag was searched for contraband candy and I attended four hours of exercise class a day, including a trampoline aerobics class where the final song was always the Time's "Jungle Love." We got to go to the frozen-yogurt chain TCBY once a week for dessert. The camp turned out to be a kind of holding pen for rich teens from the west side of Los Angeles, a few hundred miles south of where I grew up. I remember nothing about nutrition or how much weight I lost in two weeks, but I do remember learning how to fold a T-shirt like they do at Banana Republic, a skill I retain to this day. At the end of camp, we were all taken to the mall to buy new outfits with money our parents had set aside for a weight-loss makeover.

This, too, was part of the pattern—my parents investing money for me to lose weight and me always failing to maintain any kind of weight loss. There was also acupuncture and a doctor who told me that if I lost weight before my first period, I would never again struggle with my weight. In seventh grade, I belonged to a diet program that my mom drove me to every single morning before school so I could weigh in. On Halloween, my parents would pick through my candy and take some to eat for themselves, some to portion out for me. In junior high I got smart and started leaving it in my locker.

We know a lot more about dieting and childhood today than anyone did in the 1980s, when I was growing up. The American Academy of Pediatrics, for example, has cautioned both parents and doctors not to dwell too much on weight or force kids to diet; the group advises parents not even to comment on their child's weight. It turns out that focusing attention on weight is the best way to encourage a relationship to food that one might charitably call *complicated* at best, *disordered* at worst. Families should instead eat meals together and parents should focus on modeling balance in both food and exercise. Teaching healthy behavior is hard. Eating as a child is suffused with morality, even today, and it's a morality I've never given up. Beyond maybe crudités, I can't think of anything I could eat that wouldn't cause me some kind of guilt. Which is a roundabout way of saying that I have sympathy for my parents, who are now in their late sixties and no closer to enjoying peace in their own bodies or balance in their own diets.

I don't have a good answer for why I am still fat. The best I can say is that it is due to a combination of lazy food habits, a poor draw in the genetic lottery, and a love of abundance. For me to stay thin involves complete determination at the cost of a social life or fun. The flip side of abundance is scarcity, and when I diet, I immediately revert to panic mode and stop eating dinner or want to eat only salads.

One week after my fortieth birthday, in mid-July 2017, I joined Weight Watchers for the first time since the 1980s. This was two years after Jean Nidetch died and I'd learned about her life. I could say that good ideas simply keep, but the truth was I procrastinated. I knew that doing it meant I was going to have to get serious again about dieting. In the intervening two years, I tried everything else, including appointments with a celebrity diet doctor who told me I just needed to go paleo. The client after me was an A-list actor training for a part as a boxer; he looked lit from within, so perhaps that was what I needed to do as well? Paleo-boxing lasted maybe two weeks, but then I watched *The Great British Bake Off* while eating straight from a pan of Duncan Hines brownies I had baked, still warm. I wanted to think that my weight was special enough that it necessitated a special doctor, so I consulted with a physician about getting a gastric balloon, a device that, when inserted into my stomach and filled with saline, would make me feel fuller and eat less. The procedure cost around $10,000, so there was no way I could afford it, plus one potential side effect was continuous nausea. For about a month, I became a late-in-life bulimic, shoving the handle of my toothbrush down my throat to throw up, not every meal, but ice cream or cheeseburgers. None of it was particularly sane or sustainable.

I kept coming back to Jean, thinking about her as some kind of Fairy Grand-Bubbe nagging me to just give her advice a try. Years ago I'd gone to a single Weight Watchers meeting in midtown. Or rather, I tried to go. It was held in the basement of a large office building and when I went to security to show my identification, the guard took one look at me and said, "Basement?" I was crushed. Was it that obvious? I never did make it down to that meeting. Jean observed, "I watched people who came, under duress. And they would sit there with their arms folded. And I watched them unfold, and I watched them move closer, just as you are doing now, and it moved me. It still does." I guess I was ready to be moved.

The average age of a Weight Watchers member in the United States is forty-eight. This skews a little younger for members who follow the program entirely online (average age forty-five) and a little older for those who choose to go to meetings (fifty-four). Currently, the program is around

90 percent female. Weight Watchers is booming, with 3.9 million active members and 31,000 meetings around the world run by 8,300 leaders who've all lost weight on the plan, which is now just one in a crowded market of diet programs.

This time, I was going to Weight Watchers truly for myself. I decided I would shop around a bit to find the meeting that felt, I don't know, the most motivating or offered the most interesting fellow Weight Watchers. I didn't actually know what I was looking for but I had a sense I would know it when I found it.

The first meeting I tried was held on Fridays at 1:15 p.m. in the flagship Weight Watchers Center in midtown Manhattan, on the fourth floor of a dusty midcentury building on Fifty-Seventh Street. It was named the Jean Nidetch Center in 2013 for the brand's fiftieth anniversary. It's a full-time Weight Watchers space rather than a church or some other temporary venue, which is where some meetings are held, and it hosts a couple of meetings a day, often before or after work or at lunch. Weight Watchers stores aren't fancy, and this one, despite being named after Jean, is no exception; they all have an air of a permanent popup store ready to be dismantled at any moment. The furnishings are just the bare necessities: brochures, chairs (armless, perhaps to better accommodate a range of sizes), a few stacks of branded chips or protein bars and water bottles for sale. The scales are off to the side and have an extra layer of privacy—when you step on one of them, you can't see a number; it's visible only to the Weight Watchers employee weighing you, who then enters it onto a card and calculates your loss (or gain).

I got there and weighed myself for the first time in maybe four months. Two hundred and sixty-two pounds exactly, more than my father weighed, and he was about eight inches taller than my five seven. I was just a few pounds shy of my heaviest weight ever, which meant I had gained back all but three of the seventy pounds I'd lost five years earlier on a low-calorie, high-protein, low-carbohydrate diet supplemented, frankly, with a lot of meal skipping. I was what the writer Roxane Gay called "Lane Bryant fat" or what some fat-acceptance types called "small fat." What that meant to me is that sometimes I didn't fit into the largest straight-size (i.e., not plus-size) clothes and was forced to buy size 16 pants online, where most retailers' "extended sizes" were available. God forbid they should keep them in stores where their fat customers could be seen shopping. I didn't need a seat-belt extender in an airplane. I had never not fit into a chair. I had, however, broken a chair (while eating a cupcake, just before going to a club and seeing my recently ex–boyfriend making out with a skinny brunette gallerist on the dance floor). I didn't know what it was like to wear a size 22 or a 42, and to be frank, I hoped I never would. It was probably easier to exist in the world at my size than at a bigger one, but I didn't think it was easy to exist in the world at any above-ideal weight. My mother used to tell me when I was growing up that for men, there was a seventy-five-pound window before they started to be considered fat, but for women it was ten pounds.

I was saved from complete disappointment at how big I had become by the tinge of hope that I was starting over. I grabbed a bunch of instructional sheets and a Weight

Watchers pamphlet that covered the topics for each week's meeting; this one was "Focus on Fun." On the front was a back shot of a fat middle-aged white woman in a black bikini walking into what I decided was the Caribbean with her arms parallel to the sea. The importance of finding physical activity you enjoyed was broken down in a worksheet titled "What to Do: Find Your Feel-Good Moves." I sat down and read a recipe I knew I'd never make for an ancient-grain salad with chicken, peach, and tarragon. There was a skinny seventy-something woman here, Doris, with her even older husband, Ezra, who was the one trying to lose weight. Janie, a middle-aged redhead wearing a black three-piece suit who had stayed at her goal weight long enough to become a lifetime member—someone who has lost the weight and works toward maintaining it—showed Doris and Ezra the charm she'd gotten for losing thirty-five pounds. It was gold and in the shape of a key with the Weight Watchers logo stamped on it. There were other shapes—stars, coins—for losing 5 or 10 percent of one's body weight. Originally, members got a silver brooch with the logo and rhinestones, a pin Jean had designed herself, but they were no longer produced.

Our leader, Barbara Rosen, a svelte, stylish, seventy-something with a blond blowout, breezed in wearing a sundress and announced, by way of beginning the proceedings, "It's hot as hell but I'm still coming to my Weight Watchers meeting." Rosen was one of the first generation of Weight Watchers losers; she'd joined in the 1970s after gaining forty-four pounds during a bad divorce, and she missed only two meetings in the first year she joined. Most impressive was that she had maintained her weight loss for over forty years. I thought she might be my living link to Jean's era, someone who would make sure I didn't succumb to my own personal Mallomar demons. A reporter at the *New York Times* once wrote of Rosen that she had "the enthusiasm of a circus announcer." She spoke in the same vintage New York City accent as Jean.

I had heard that a lot of old-timers came to her meetings as a check-in, and my fantasy was that the veteran attendees would take to me so I could understand dieting in decades past but also, hopefully, learn what it really took to keep the weight off. And maybe model life beyond forty for me. The meeting was slightly chaotic; a cell phone rang and someone yelled to turn it off. Two women in the front kept talking to each other about their grandchildren until someone behind them told them to shut up. I was the youngest person here by one generation, maybe two. This meeting had been a good idea in theory, but I was out of place.

Rosen began to discuss her recent weekend out on Long Island at a family barbecue. "You have to be very, very selective. Even when offered a doughnut." There was a chorus of murmurs about everyone loving doughnuts. Rosen continued, "They are thirteen points. If it was Häagen-Dazs I would have eaten it, but I'm not going to eat a thirteen-point doughnut in the sun standing up. I'm a food snob! It wasn't what I love. Forty-four pounds ago I would've eaten it." Mirah, a not particularly thin woman in a paisley caftan who had been on the plan since 1982, was set off by the very mention of ice cream. She almost shouted to the dozen of us assembled, "Don't get fooled, yogurt is ice cream!

Bloomingdale's yogurt down the street is seventeen points!" She reminded me of Charlton Heston screaming, "Soylent Green is people!" Mirah's warning segued into a discussion of the points value of dried fruit over fresh fruit. I heard Ezra whispering to his wife, "Apricots…apricots." I had to stop myself from giggling at the level of passion displayed over the pitfalls of food.

At the end of the meeting, those of us who were new—just Ezra and me—stayed so Rosen could go over the plan with us, although with no food off-limits, there was not a lot to explain. I could use the app on my phone to track what I ate to stay within my allotted thirty-eight points. Incidentally, the two most tracked items in Weight Watchers are beverages—coffee (which has no points when drunk black) and wine, which is four points for a four-ounce serving. Rosen carried a laminated "before" photo of herself and showed it to us to prove her former heft. Ezra asked her how many people gained the weight back. She said it wouldn't happen to him, "not if you keep coming and following the program. It's for life; you're never finished." That felt ominous. Spending my Friday afternoons kibitzing with women older than my mom about frozen yogurt and tracking every morsel I put in my mouth? I couldn't tell if that was good or bad. It was a deer-in-the-headlights moment. We think of our freedom as hard-earned, and a plan is difficult because it feels like giving up that freedom.

CHAPTER THREE

FAT IS JUST WHO I AM

1947

On her wedding day, April 20, 1947, Jean Nidetch wore a size 18 navy-blue dress with a bustle and the sides let out. She had dieted her way down from a size 20 and she was thrilled. The pattern was fixed; she would lose twenty or thirty pounds on various crash diets, drinking nothing but black coffee or eating just eggs or trying something she'd read in a magazine, like the grapefruit diet. But one can't live on citrus alone, and when she'd start to eat her favorite foods again, the pounds crept on. Whenever she asked Marty if she looked fat, he would say, "You're perfect, honey." He was a big guy too, after all, but he also meant it—he really liked the way Jean looked. This weight problem was a battle Jean waged with herself.

The wedding of Jean and Marty was a modest affair of around fifty people at a temple near her grandmother's house in Brooklyn. Buying accessories was less fraught than fitting into a dress, so Jean went overboard at a shop on Utica Avenue, buying an enormous beige cartwheel wedding hat for thirty dollars, far more than she could afford. The film-noir star and fellow Brooklyn native Barbara Stanwyck was related to a friend of Jean's, and that friend lent her a pair of Stanwyck's gloves as a lucky "something borrowed."

Marty and Jean's honeymoon ended up being a road trip because Marty had gotten a job at a department store in Tulsa, Oklahoma. They left Brooklyn the day after their wedding and drove across country in their used 1942 Buick convertible, planning their route around fairs and diners where they could eat meat loaf and milkshakes and fried eggs as they made their way west. Once they arrived, they settled into a furnished room in a house owned by another couple. Jean wasn't much of a cook, so she and Marty mostly subsisted on a diet of cold cuts, chips, pretzels, and chocolate pudding from a mix, although sometimes they'd take advantage of the air-conditioning and giant portions in restaurants. Eventually they moved into a place of their own where they could fully indulge their sweet tooth. Jean baked cakes for dessert or they'd go for a walk after dinner and get ice cream or drive up to a watermelon stand that would serve them as they sat in their convertible.

Jean was a woman of her era; she worked until she got married, then became a full-time housewife. Six million women were in the workforce during the war, and half of them left immediately after it ended, in 1945. The 1950s were a return to domesticity and traditional gender roles. Men came back from the war and went to work, and women stayed home to raise children and care for the household.

Brides were young; in 1956, the median age for a first-time bride was twenty. The comforts of the suburbs—two-car garages and nuclear families and home appliances—were celebrated. By 1960, only about 35 percent of women worked outside the home, and their pay averaged just 60 cents for every dollar earned by men. In *The Feminine Mystique,* her critique of the domestic roles of the postwar era, Betty Friedan wrote of housewives zombified, living their mind-numbing lives without a hint of personal ambition. "Their only dream was to be perfect wives and mothers; their highest ambition to have five children and a beautiful house, their only fight to get and keep their husbands. They had no thought for the unfeminine problems of the world outside the home; they wanted the men to make the major decisions. They gloried in their role as women, and wrote proudly on the census blank: 'Occupation: housewife.'"

Jean would sometimes get bored of housewifery and take the bus to downtown Tulsa in her beige wedding hat and go to the department stores. She liked to tell women browsing that she was a saleswoman. She, somewhat strangely, figured that since she had been lying about her weight so long, it had prepped her to be great at fibbing in any number of ways. And besides, her sunny demeanor won everyone over. She knew how to politely tell someone if the dress she was trying on made her hips look big or if the color didn't suit her, and she would then get her phone number and promise to call if she saw anything arrive on the floor that would work for her. This was her first inkling that she could be a winning salesperson; soon, she was a modern-day personal stylist, recommending clothes and charging a commission for her service.

In the fashion of the era, the hourglass figure was all the rage, clothes with nipped-in waists, full skirts, and soft shoulders. It was both a celebration of and a reaction to the moment, marking the end of wartime rations (the rubber business resumed around this point to create the merry widow and other shapewear necessary to popularize the look) and a return to abundance. It showed femininity as soft, maybe even a little impractical. This feminine ideal trickled down into children's culture too. Disney's animated heroines became increasingly lithe from 1950s Cinderella on; Barbie and her impossibly buxom figure debuted in 1959. On the relatively new medium of television, Jack LaLanne, who had opened up some of the country's first gyms in 1936, had his own fitness show debut in 1951. It was on the air until 1985.

Home economics classes of the postwar years advocated working within the home, depicting it as a challenging and fulfilling role. It was a popular class across the country; a study by the Educational Testing Service found that eleventh-grade girls ranked home ec, as it was commonly called, as their number-one area of interest in high school. A degree in home economics could lead to a career in teaching or at a food company. (Many of these companies employed fictional home economists as corporate mascots. The most famous was Betty Crocker, but there were also Mary Alden at Quaker Oats, Mary Blake at Carnation, Patricia Collier at Dole, Ann Pillsbury at Pillsbury, and Kay Kellogg at Kellogg.) A typical high-school home economics curriculum covered how to shop for your family and presented traditional divisions of labor down gender lines (yard work and barbecuing for Dad and everything else for Mom), since it was no longer common for middle-class households to employ full-time domestic help. A home ec lesson plan from Alabama in the early 1960s instructs teachers to "discuss how food 'becomes us.' Look at contrasting pictures of persons showing fat and thin, calm and nervous, happy and unhappy, ruddy and pale, energetic and weary, lustrous lively hair and dull hair. Recognize that all foods eaten daily 'become you' and all foods eaten are to be considered as one's diet for the day."

Luckily for Jean and other harried housewives, the food industry was prepared to help them in the kitchen, touting convenience foods such as cake mixes (which came on the market in 1947), nondairy creamer (1952), Pillsbury's signature crack-on-the-line dough packaging (patented in 1952), and Eggo frozen waffles and Cheez Whiz (both 1953), all symbols of cultural innovation and scientific achievement. It was cooking without the senses, as the food writer Laura Shapiro wrote in her book *Something from the Oven*. "Nutrients and calories bid for attention; standardized equipment and measurements took the place of impressionistic cupfuls; and sanitation became the most demanding deity in the nation's culinary pantheon." The message was, to quote Pillsbury's motto, "Nothing says lovin' like something from the oven." It just didn't matter what means it took to get dinner (or dessert or a snack) on the table.

Foods made in factories had begun to enter into American homes in the nineteenth century, but they flooded the market in the 1950s, with the might of the food industry and even politicians behind them. Shortly after his 1953 inauguration, President Dwight Eisenhower attended a luncheon to celebrate so-called miracle foods, including frozen vegetables, red meat raised with hormones and antibiotics, and powdered orange-juice concentrate. In 1954, when two-thirds of American families owned a television, Swanson launched its first TV dinner, an homage to Thanksgiving with turkey, cornbread stuffing, peas, and sweet potatoes that cost 98 cents. The company sold ten million of them that year. If you wanted to eat out, the 1950s saw the birth of the fast-food chain. Dunkin' Donuts in 1950; Taco Bell in 1952; Burger King in 1954; McDonald's in 1955; Kentucky Fried Chicken in 1955; Pizza Hut in 1958; International House of Pancakes in 1958; Domino's Pizza in 1960. A steady parade of caloric greatest hits.

Poppy Cannon, a writer at the society magazine *Town and Country*, wrote the 1951 bestselling *Can-Opener Cookbook*. A recipe for casserole à la king called for canned chicken à la king, canned macaroni in cream sauce with cream cheese, bread crumbs, butter, and parsley or watercress for garnish (Cannon thought the way food was presented made all the difference). The magazine *Better Homes and Gardens* published its first story on microwave cooking in 1957. Peg Bracken, a copywriter in Portland, Oregon, published her *I Hate to Cook Book* in 1960, and it went on to sell three million copies. Bracken's recipes relied on bouillon cubes, canned soup, and a healthy dose of dry wit. The recipe for Skid Road Stroganoff is a two-line poem: "Brown the garlic, onion, and crumbled beef in the oil. Add the flour, salt, paprika, and mushrooms, stir, and let cook five minutes while you light a cigarette and stare sullenly at the sink." These women, including writers like Shirley Jackson (*Life Among the Savages*), Jean Kerr (*Please*

Don't Eat the Daisies), and the journalist Erma Bombeck (who wrote a syndicated column about being a housewife called At Wit's End), didn't say that women should reject the home but they exposed domestic bliss as a fabrication. Convenience was subversive for women who were supposed to find their calling in the kitchen.

In January of 1948, Jean and Marty moved across the country again, this time to Warren in western Pennsylvania, so he could take a job as the manager of a furniture store. They lived in an apartment next door to two cherubic spinsters who welcomed them with a plate of cookies still warm from the oven, and Jean instantly felt at home. But there was even less for her to do in Warren than there'd been in Oklahoma. If you liked to go canoeing in the summer and sledding in the winter, there was plenty to keep you occupied, but the Nidetches were native New Yorkers who didn't do athleticism; their favorite pastimes (when not dining out) were shopping and going to the movies. So they kept eating. They threw dinner parties and picnics and teas. They made friends with the Greek owners of the café across the street from Marty's store who supplied them with flaky, nutty pastries.

Jean and Marty were popular because they made great guests. They ate everything with gusto and were quick to lavish compliments on the stunning roast chicken or the neat icing on a cake. They also gained weight together; Jean felt that she'd have nothing to wear to temple because none of her dresses could zip up, nor could Marty's pants. Once she even wore drapes to a costume party because nothing else fit. Maybe they were fat, but it was because they were so happy.

Looking back, she said, "Of course, I can tell you that we can say the hell with it, we're going to be how we are and we don't care. But deep down, there is a part of every fat person that does care—it's a pose, a pretense based on denial." They were conscious of being the jolly fat couple, ready to make a joke at their own expense to keep someone else from doing it. "I'm glandular," she said as part of her repartee, glands being a strangely popular excuse for being overweight in the midcentury. Or: "I'm big-boned. One of my aunts was very stout, even if she wasn't a blood relative." Jean found this old comic routine a sad and rather pathetic party trick, no more amusing than the guest who gets drunk and puts a lampshade on his head.

What Jean wanted was a child. It took two years of trying for her to get pregnant, and when she did, both her mother and mother-in-law came to Warren to help out—it would be the first grandchild for them both. Jean's doctor decided to induce labor when she was sick for two weeks at the very end of her pregnancy. The labor and birth seemed to go along fine but the next morning when she awoke, Jean knew instantly that there was bad news. She thought it was her fault the baby hadn't lived; she went into a state of shock, losing her hearing for a week. Marty converted some of his GI life insurance so Jean and her mother could go to Florida to recuperate and focus on her health. It was there Jean met another young woman who had lost a child. Talking about it was cathartic and a consolation. Discussing her experience with someone who knew exactly what she was going through changed her life. Jean made the connection that even if you were dealing with the most difficult thing that had ever happened to you, talking with someone who shared your pain helped you get through it.

She got pregnant again, in 1951, and had her first son, David. When she got up to feed him in the middle of the night, she'd get herself a snack. That snacking habit lasted long after David was sleeping through the night. Jean and Marty missed family and home and decided to move back to New York City when David was two months old. After shuttling between their parents' homes for a year, they found an apartment in Deepdale Gardens in northeast Queens, right on the border of Long Island. Jean and Marty were the real-life Honeymooners. He drove a bus and she stayed at home, but when money was tight, Jean would go to her aunt's chicken farm in New Jersey and bring back eggs to sell door-to-door. Getting invited into people's homes for coffee and cake was a fringe benefit. And Jean Nidetch the saleswoman knew better than to refuse. Once, when Marty was hired as a driver for a limousine, she asked him, "Don't you ever want to sit in the backseat?" He told her, "You have to understand, Jean, some people never sit in the backseat." She thought to herself, *I want to be the passenger in a limo.*

When she got pregnant again, in 1956, Jean weighed 190 pounds. Her doctor told her that if she didn't lose weight, she might have some cardiac damage, and she was terrified of losing another baby. Pregnancy, like a crash diet, was a painful experience that Jean thought you had to suffer through. She decided to take appetite suppressants during her pregnancy, and she lost thirty pounds before giving birth. She was relieved her son Richard was born without any side effects from the drugs, although he would later point out that his first baby teeth did come in rotten.

Thus began another cycle of losing twenty to thirty pounds from fasting or Metrecal or other liquid diets or guzzling No-Cal diet soda or mysterious weekly injections from a doctor in New Jersey who promised her they would allow her to eat anything she wanted (until she fainted in the street from dehydration). She took oil pills, ate wafers that looked and tasted like dog biscuits, and sometimes subsisted on black coffee and cigarettes. She even went to a hypnotist. Whenever Jean began a new diet, Marty would shake his head and mutter, "Not again." The whole family suffered when she was trying to lose weight. "Anyone living on celery and carrot sticks has a right to feel miserable," she said. Jean thought she could rely on sheer willpower, but she cheated all the time, either raiding the refrigerator under the veil of night to make a halvah sandwich or seeking out her stash of Mallomars in the bathroom. As a kid, Richard thought that every household kept Fig Newtons and Oreos under the sink. Jean wasn't exactly demonstrating healthy habits to her sons, although dieting and obesity were still mostly the domain of adults rather than children. Dr. Benjamin Spock, the prevailing childrearing expert of the time, wrote that being mildly overweight was common from the age of seven until the early teenage years, but kids would likely lose the pounds without much effort by the time they were fifteen.

A 1953 pamphlet called "Eat and Get Slim" provided menus for quick weight loss that featured such diet staples as grapefruits and bouillon. There were illustrated exercises for the bosom and fatty knees. Cigarettes to curb appetite were encouraged. ("You can't eat cigarettes but in a pinch they can serve as food until something better comes along.") The gelatin company Knox had its own diet plan, as did Ry-Krisp crackers, a plan promoted by a cartoon Sherlock character called Weight-Watcher, "your man when it comes to cracking the case of the Creeping Pound." By 1959, ninety-two diet books were in print, including titles such as Dr. Herman Taller's 1961 *Calories Don't Count* (its endorsement of a specific manufacturer's safflower-oil supplements led to a grand jury investigation that resulted in Taller's being indicted in 1967 for mail fraud, conspiracy, and violation of the Food, Drug and Cosmetic Act) and Sidney Petrie's *Martinis and Whipped Cream*, a low-carbohydrate diet. By 1961, 40 percent of Americans used low-calorie products.

At the end of the 1950s, Jean was resigned to a lifetime of frustration. She was jealous of any woman who was smaller than her; think of her old teenage habit of wanting to befriend only those bigger than her. If Marty dared to suggest she buy a dress he saw on a skinny woman, she would seethe and tell herself that no dress could create the illusion of being a hundred pounds slimmer. One or two such skinny women even had the nerve to approach Jean and say, "Honey, with a face like yours, how could you let yourself go like that?" She never did have much of a comeback to that, maybe coming up with a cliché like "But there's more of me to love!" She overheard other people describing her as "that fat woman," "the pleasant woman who has a little weight to lose," "that rather large woman," and "the chubby woman." "Am I as fat as that woman?" she'd ask her husband at a party. "Oh, no," he'd say. "You're taller. You carry your weight better." At least, Jean reasoned, her husband loved her. And thin women would age faster, since they didn't have any fullness in their faces. Jean didn't feel like she had let herself go; rather, she felt that being fat was who she was. The rush of going on a diet followed by the sting of failure that came after falling off it left her feeling helpless. "When I reached that 214 pounds, I was so demoralized and I almost decided to give up and just accept the fact that I was going to be an FF—'fatty forever.' Fat is an ugly word and it made me feel ugly. I knew I had to do something about it because the description would haunt me until I did."

CHAPTER FOUR

SHARING IS ON A VOLUNTARY BASIS

August 2017

I dressed in my lightest one-piece workout jumpsuit for my first Weight Watchers weigh-in, a week after I started the program. I looked like an athleisure version of Humpty Dumpty in it, but it weighed almost nothing. No bra, no underwear—as little clothing as I could get away with in public without violating decency laws. I removed my tiny hoop earrings and abstained from morning coffee and water—nothing would impinge on the victory of my week of effort.

I'd quickly realized that all meetings followed more or less the same structure: You come in a few minutes before it starts and get in line to get weighed. You strip off as many layers as you can. (Like me, a lot of people wore workout clothes, regardless of whether they had plans to exercise, because they were so light. Some people wore jeans or whatever they'd had on at work, although leaders swore they'd seen women take off their bras. All of us took off our shoes and coats, though.

Some meeting spaces even had little booths where you could do the whole thing behind a cubicle wall or curtain.) You're then given a name tag and you find a seat. The leader, standing and facing everyone, makes some remarks about the week. If there's been a heat wave or a holiday or something else that might affect people's eating habits, she talks about that. And then there's the weekly handout, which you get when you weigh in. It covers health or food or wellness and, in theory, dictates what Weight Watchers members all over the country talk about that week. Some leaders stick to the program's official topic, some make a perfunctory mention of it, and others ignore it entirely in favor of whatever they or their members want to talk about. Sharing is on a voluntary basis; some members talk all the time about the minutiae of their lives, while others come every week and never say a word. Some meetings are held midday in business centers and filled with office workers eating lunch who leave as soon as it's over, and others are in the late afternoon and full of retirees who all go out for coffee after and seem to be genuine friends. Supposedly there's one near the theater district in Manhattan where all the Broadway actors and dancers go but I've never figured out which one it is. Some meetings are known for being macro about feelings or themes and others tend to be more in the weeds, people talking about recipes, food hacks, specific point values. Some leaders come across like motivational speakers; others are like group therapists. After half an hour, people share celebrations and get stickers or little charms for things they're proud of, like going on a trip and not gaining weight or going from an obese BMI to just overweight. And that's it. New members stay for a few minutes so the leader can go over the plan, and other people will hang around to ask the leader questions or share a victory privately. The whole thing lasts about forty-five minutes. The good leaders will remind you as you're leaving to take off your name tag, otherwise you run the risk of having your name and the Weight Watchers logo affixed to your chest until someone is kind enough to tell you it's there.

After just a week on the program I was already tired of all the food in my apartment and bored with cooking healthy things for myself. Smoked trout and salad for lunch is not so bad, but I kept wondering if I could keep this up. Or was the question, did I want to? I thought I was showing real restraint eating a not very satisfying diet ice cream sandwich and then I looked it up and found it had six points out of the just thirty-something I was allotted for the entire day. I spent half an hour in bed past midnight watching videos on Instagram's discover page of this blond woman who baked things like cookies in skillets served hot and topped with mounds of ice cream. I guess that was my porn now.

I decided that, as much as I loved a living link to Jean, and even though Barbara Rosen was a kind of talisman, her meeting just wasn't for me. As amusing as her loyal crew was, they were decades and decades older than me. I was looking for people talking about emotion and body image and a group that was more diverse in age, race, life experience— I needed a different kind of support to get through this year. So I started shopping around. I dropped by a late-morning meeting deep in a building in Manhattan's financial district. The Weight Watchers program at the time was called Beyond the Scale, but I should admit the scale was still the most important element for me. I weighed myself and found I'd lost 2.1 pounds. I knew I should have been happy, but I was ready for some big first-week loss, at least 5 pounds, even if it was just water weight, whatever that was.

That meeting's leader was a fifty-something gay man who was talking about how he kept his largest pair of pants "to keep me honest." I couldn't stay after the weigh-in, though. I was writing a profile of the actress Busy Philipps and had to attend a SoulCycle class with her. It's funny, or maybe tragic, that although she's lauded in Hollywood for having a more real or relatable body and being honest about gaining weight and about how hard she diets and exercises to keep herself thin, when you see her in person, her body is insane, by which I mean lean and toned beyond what anyone would reasonably call "relatable."

After the SoulCycle class, we both ate grain bowls and I told her I was doing Weight Watchers. She got me to share banana bread with her. "This is how I do it for my kids," she said, and she proceeded to cut it into a grid pattern so we could eat tiny little bites. The thing is, I'd prefer to wolf down something like banana bread in private. Sharing it and eating it slowly in the presence of another person makes me feel self-conscious and somehow dampens my enjoyment of it. Even though lunches are the default activity for an interview, I would rather not eat while working. Eating is for comfort and enjoyment, not work.

I hadn't found my people at any of the meetings so far, so I kept looking. I did a bit of research online and found a Sunday meeting in Park Slope, in Brooklyn, that a lot of people seemed to like, and I decided to try it.

I took a shared Uber there and the driver had navigation on. As I got into the packed car, the GPS robot voice said, loud and clear, "Destination is Weight Watchers Park Slope." I was mortified.

The meeting was in a retail space on the ground floor of a building that also hosted a SoulCycle basically upstairs. I couldn't tell if this was the most convenient combination ever or evidence of a life lived slightly deranged. SoulCycle is emblematic of the new way of wellness—you're paying close to forty dollars to have an instructor talk to you about how much inner strength you have while you're sweating. Thirty years ago, there could have been a Jazzercise there. The workout details change but the paradigm doesn't. The cost of SoulCycle is in marked contrast to that of Weight Watchers, which, depending on where you live, runs around ten dollars a week.

The Park Slope meeting room was the size of a boutique or maybe a small restaurant; there was a counter where you could buy gum and three-point cake mixes designed to be made and microwaved in mugs. There was also significantly more seating than I'd seen in any previous Weight Watchers location, which spoke to the popularity of the leader, Miriam, who ran two meetings here every Sunday morning. Miriam was unlike any Weight Watchers leader I had ever seen, or even imagined. She was a vegan Jewish mom in her late forties, a native New Yorker, and today she wore a polka-dot dress and had blue ombre hair (which she said was sometimes also platinum, sometimes also pink or purple). She had tattoos of skulls and roses and Hebrew script, all acquired after she'd lost the weight. She hadn't grown up fat like me; in fact, she'd been a competitive gymnast who trained four hours a day, four days a week. When she quit, at age seventeen, she'd gained fifteen pounds in a month. She was eating because she was depressed, relieved, and dealing with chaos in her family life. But she had been so small to begin with that fifteen pounds just meant she started to look like an average teenager. By the time she left to go to college in Southern California, she was a normal weight—she could maybe have lost five or ten pounds—but then she ate her way through the next four years, gaining thirty pounds or so. She and her future husband met in college and married soon after graduation, and, like Jean, at her wedding she wore the best dress she could find in her size.

The turning point was a few years later, when she signed up one of her two young daughters for gymnastics. "We get there at eight forty-five and I take off her sweatpants and her little jacket and sneakers and I put them in a cubby and there she is with her little pigtails and her bangs and her whole black leotard. She just wandered off with the teacher and I looked and burst into tears," Miriam said. "The woman standing next to me saw that I was crying and tapped me and she's like, 'Is it your daughter's first day?' And I was like, yes." The woman told her she had cried at her daughter's first day too. "She had no clue I [was crying because I] saw my reflection. I was like, when I was four, I ran in and I did it and this is what I've become. I'm the fat mom, out here, looking in. How did I let this happen? I was so disappointed, I was angry with myself." Worse yet, the man who owned the gym had been one of Miriam's gymnastic coaches and she was afraid he would recognize her. Or what if she had gained so much weight, he didn't? She joined Weight Watchers after that, in November 2000, when she was about to turn thirty-one. In seventeen weeks she lost fifty-five pounds.

This meeting, one of several she led around Brooklyn each week, was packed with dozens of people, and they were truly a cross-section of the city: a group of Orthodox Jewish women, black teenagers, a middle-aged white lesbian couple losing weight together, and a stay-at-home mom who looked like the actor Brie Larson and who had lost 103 pounds. There was a fifty-something judge, Patrice, a black woman with short hair who was trying to lose the fifty pounds she'd gained with her children. The children were now adults, and she joked, "That's how long I've put off dieting and been unhappy."

There was a woman named Rosemarie who lived with her parents in Bensonhurst, where *Saturday Night Fever* was filmed. She worked nights as a nurse and had gained weight grazing on food during her shift. Her dream was to join the air force, and, at thirty, she'd gone to a recruiter. He'd asked her height and weight. She told him she was five foot three and didn't know her weight. He said that the limit for her height was 155 pounds. She figured maybe she was 170 at the most and stepped on their scale. She'd weighed 237 pounds. Now she was 190. She was following Miriam's advice to "lose one pound seventy times." She had long, curly brown hair she wore swept back in a ponytail and she dressed like a dad in the 1990s: an aggressively neat pair of khaki pants with a polo shirt tucked into them and chunky white sneakers. She was the kind of girl who raised her hand to answer every question in class. I couldn't tell if I was annoyed by her, intimidated by her, or wanted her to be my dieting muse. Probably all three.

Weight Watchers is nothing if not literal, so that week we were asked to write down three things "beyond the scale" that made us happy. That part was difficult for me to get inspired by. I felt like I was above worksheets, but I forced myself to go along with it. If I was going to be here for an hour on a Sunday morning, I might as well make the most of the experience. I thought for a while about what made me happy and wrote down the first three things that popped into my head: *my Nespresso machine, walking Joan to the park,* and *sheet masks.* I was annoyed because I felt like I was smarter than a dumb list, but I was also annoyed that my list seemed vapid. "What is the difference between defining and describing our lives with regard to weight?" Miriam asked. That was her final thought before people shared celebrations, which felt like a holdover from Jean's era. People talked about weight-loss milestones; a police-man named Royce noted that he'd lost six pounds this week. I left knowing I could get behind this meeting and, in particular, this leader.

The only time I've ever been thin—indisputably thin, in the way I've always dreamed of—was for a few short years in high school. This was achieved primarily through starvation eased by drugs. Not a pill casually popped but lines of cocaine and methamphetamine the length of a CD case that simply eliminated the part of my brain that felt hunger for days on end. The first time I was ever offered drugs I was fifteen and at a party in a ranch house near where I went to school. My friend Magdalena and I might have been the only high-school girls there—some guys who worked at a local record store had invited us. I have no idea where the drugs came from, but the two of us were crowded in a half-bath, taking turns peeing while we talked about the cute young janitor from our school who was there, and then Magdalena unfolded a white piece of paper carefully, like origami in reverse. The cocaine inside was the same cream color as the walls of my bedroom. Magdalena set about making even lines of it with her driver's license, which she had just earned maybe three weeks prior. She rolled up a dollar bill and we got to work snorting it. She and I left the bathroom and sat on the floor, our backs to a wall. I was wearing a yellowing plain V-neck T-shirt and could feel the blood pulsing and was suddenly aware of the forward thrust of my clavicle.

Collarbones were big that year when we all wanted to be waifs. One morning in the school library, Magdalena had ripped out a photo of Amber Valletta from *Vogue*, her clavicle a curly bracket on its side. I felt awake, fragile, and not hungry. It was the first time I felt beautiful. The fact that I didn't eat for a full twenty-four hours after that helped too, and soon drugs became the secret hero of my high-school weight-loss journey. I wanted to be thin so bad that the potential dangers didn't even occur to me. After a few years, when I felt like I was relying on the drugs to stay thin, I was able to walk away from them. It's interesting that this was easy to do, both mentally and physically, whereas dieting was so much more of a struggle.

My thin odyssey had begun at the end of my freshman year of high school, when I weighed 166 pounds and still hadn't gone through a final growth spurt. I went to Europe for the first time, tagging along with my father and stepmother on a business trip, my grandmother coming along to babysit me while they were in meetings, even though I felt like I was too old to have a minder. She mostly sat in cafés chain-smoking More Menthol 120's and eating dried fruit she had brought with her from San Francisco while I devised how best to spend the hundred dollars I had. I tried on a ribbed horizontally striped sweater at the French chain Kookaï and, for a moment, glimpsed what I hoped would be the elegance of my future. That was interrupted by a saleswoman saying in her French-accented English, "For you, I don't think stripes." You know what they say about fat people and horizontal stripes. There are rules for us.

It wasn't that one humiliation that flipped the switch, but somewhere between my freshman and sophomore years, I lost forty pounds. That summer I embarked on a diet of my own invention that involved eating two plain bagels and drinking a quart of orange juice over the course of the morning and then fasting for the rest of the day. I chugged the distilled water that my mother bought by the gallon—she believed spring water was all marketing—to fill myself up and took walks around the harbor.

Denial, particularly self-denial, is its own kind of pleasure. While I wouldn't call my family entirely abstemious, my parents have always been much better at controlling their appetites than me. Or maybe food was just my oblivion and theirs was something else. I like a plan; I thrive on forward motion. A diet isn't just a diet but a fantasy, an investment in the future self. Diet culture and weight loss are directly related to the Protestant work ethic in America. I wasn't brought up Protestant—my mom decided at some point in the late 1980s she was Wiccan, and my dad once told me his religion is Big Sur—but I was raised with the concept of always working. If you weren't in school, you were interning or you had a job. Productivity is its own prize.

I started a new school in tenth grade, a prep school whose dining hall I was tethered to and whose mystery-meat lunches I refused to touch. This being the 1990s, there was an all-you-can-eat fat-free frozen-yogurt machine, vanilla or chocolate, complete with wafer cones. Many of my female classmates picked at salads and subsisted on high-sugar, fat-free desserts: Red Vines, SnackWell's devil's food cookies, plain bread that we toasted in a giant communal toaster that was a kind of temporary autonomous zone where everyone made small talk with each other. It's clear in retrospect that many of the girls at school were probably suffering from the same pressures to be thin, to study all the time, to get into the college of their choice. We talked about all of those things, but not food. No one talked about diets. We wanted our lives to seem effortless; dieting was slightly embarrassing.

It was 1992, the same year the food pyramid debuted as a way for Americans to understand what made up a healthy diet. My own diet consisted of veggie burgers every other Friday, which was when the dining hall churned out the one meal that I liked; oatmeal with tons of brown sugar for breakfast; and baked potatoes sliced into wedges and dipped in ketchup that I convinced myself tasted just like french fries. (They most certainly did not.) The saddest birthday cake I ever requested was a fat-free one from Entenmann's that came in a box. I ate a lot of lollipops and chewed a lot of gum, which seemed like a sexy way to distract myself from hunger. I dabbled in cigarettes, but we always had to smoke them in groups with the shaggy-haired boys who procured them and who would always taunt me because I didn't know how to inhale. That embarrassment kept me from really taking on that vice. I was down to 125 before the holidays of my sophomore year. I wore a size 4.

Maybe the eating disorder was always there. First, I copied my mother's habit of abstaining from dinner. My school required some kind of sports three days a week, but those of us uninterested in sports could run a mile around the track or take yoga. One spring the school even offered self-defense. Exercise was an afterthought. Then there were the appetite-suppressing and digestion-boosting tricks. I found laxatives in a drawer in the kitchen at my dad's house and started taking those semiregularly, and then there were the drugs to distract me from how hungry and tired I was.

My goal weight was 115 pounds, a number I picked completely at random but that seemed sufficiently small that, if I managed to reach it, no one would ever consider me fat again. I never did see that number on my scale. I did get to 119 after a particularly bad flu and I remember my stepmother congratulating me on all the weight I had lost. Everyone congratulated me on being thin at last because I'm sure I seemed like I was doing well. I had lost weight and got good grades and had a nice group of friends. There was no reason to suspect anything was wrong.

And it's not like I opened up and told anyone, not my family or even my friends. I thought it was something I had to do in secret, particularly because I was known at school as an outspoken feminist. I organized celebrations for Women's History Month and was voted Most Likely to Lead a Revolution. My social life revolved around going to see feminist punk bands like Bikini Kill sing, "As a woman I was taught to always be hungry." I understood that I was a product of society and yet I was ashamed I couldn't rise above it, that my ideals weren't enough to stop me from constantly thinking about my weight.

But here's the thing: Even though I was definitely thin—skinny, even—I wasn't transformed. My expectations from fantasies and young-adult novels that I would change from the outside in, that I would stop feeling like an awkward fat girl, that I would love what I saw in the mirror, that I would stop craving grilled cheese sandwiches and nachos, didn't come true. I didn't go to prom. I didn't have a boyfriend. I wrote about how invisible I was to boys every night in my journal and then signed off with *I will survive*. I touched my hip bones a lot before I went to sleep in my twin Ikea bed. I later read that Jean did that too after she lost the weight. They were a novelty for both of us. My personality has always skewed more to the Wife of Bath or Miss Piggy side of outrageousness than the mysterious or intriguing pretty girl. I was the smart one, not the pretty one. If the unruly body is the opposite of the docile body, why did I want to be docile, anyway?

CHAPTER FIVE

WE ALL WANT MIRACLES

1961

You have to make the decision to lose weight in your head, not your stomach," Jean said. It's the kind of buckle-down advice that is far easier said than done, but it's what she essentially did. It was the fall of 1961, Jean was thirty-eight years old, stood five foot seven inches, and weighed 214 pounds. After that well-meaning neighbor in the supermarket mistakenly thought she was pregnant, Jean had had enough angst about her weight.

There was a free obesity clinic in Manhattan at the Bureau of Nutrition of the New York City Department of Health. (In 1962, just 13 percent of American adults were clinically obese, and the fact that there were free dieting courses combining support and education offered by local government is an interesting contrast to today.) Jean lied and said she weighed 315 pounds when she made the appointment because she was worried she might not be obese enough to qualify.

Turned out she was fat enough. She took two buses and the subway to get there, dressed in a big, flared coat to hide her body. Everyone in the waiting area was fat and seemed angry. Many of them were hiding behind sunglasses.

She sat down in the last row and listened to the speaker, a thin, severe nutritionist Jean called Miss Jones. (She perceived Miss Jones as someone who couldn't have ever been fat and who wouldn't understand her plight. In response, Jean would later stipulate that all Weight Watchers franchise holders must be members and willing to display life-size pictures of themselves from their fat days.) After weighing the new member, Miss Jones told Jean her target weight was 142 pounds. *A hundred and forty-two pounds!* Jean thought. She would have been happy to weigh 175. Even on her driver's license she had lied and said 145 pounds, which was less than she had ever weighed as an adult. "But look at me, I'm big-boned," she said in protest. "You're not," Miss Jones replied. "You have a medium frame, and you will weigh one hundred and forty-two pounds. You're not to question. You're not to judge. You will follow my instructions and eat the foods listed on the handout I'm going to give you."

Jean was put on a prudent diet for cardiac health developed by obesity researcher Dr. Norman Jolliffe, who had died just a few weeks earlier, in August 1961, right before his sixtieth birthday. He'd opened his first clinic in 1945 and written *Reduce and Stay Reduced* and *The Reducing Guide* in the early 1950s. He was also ahead of his time as a crusader for nutritious school lunches, writing that "a peanut butter sandwich, milk, half an apple, and a strip of green pepper do not make a lunch for a growing child." (By contemporary standards, this sounds exceptionally healthy.) The diet Jean was put on was developed from Jolliffe's 1957 study of eleven hundred men in what he termed an Anti-Coronary Club. It was specific and inflexible: Fish five times a week and two pieces of bread and two glasses of milk per day. Liver once a week was compulsory.

At each weekly weigh-in, Jean peppered Miss Jones with questions about possible swaps. If she didn't eat breakfast, could she eat a double lunch? What if she didn't have any dairy for six days and had a milkshake on the seventh? Could she have the occasional corn muffin instead of bread? The answer was no, no, always no. There was no meal skipping, no doubling up, no substitutions, no place for sweets, no alcohol, and if you didn't stick to the plan, you were asked to leave. Jean was informed that she was supposed to lose exactly two pounds nine ounces a week. (Today, most commercial diet programs hesitate to tell anyone how much to lose and will state that one to two pounds per week is a realistic and healthy rate of weight loss.) Jean lost just two pounds the first week, which she saw as a less-than-total victory. "I want that nine ounces," she joked. She cheated sometimes—those Mallomars stuffed in the bathroom hamper were still there and she'd throw the wrappers out in shame when Marty and the boys weren't home. But she stuck with the program. She even started making a concoction of her required two glasses of milk blended with lots of ice and a dash of vanilla extract. She ate it with a spoon, pretending it was a malted milkshake, though it surely tasted nothing like one. Maybe it was all that saying no to everything she had once loved that felt delicious. After ten weeks, she had lost twenty pounds.

The diet she was on—was that a way to live? Our culture, then as now, rewarded the dieter, no matter how regimented a lifestyle that meant committing to. Jean joined the obesity clinic during the first year of the presidency of John F. Kennedy, a time when youth, vigor, and physical fitness felt as fresh as the First Family. The First Lady, Jacqueline Kennedy, was fond of wearing tailored shifts or fitted little suits rather than the forgiving full skirts of the 1950s, which suddenly looked matronly, and everyday women wanted to emulate her. But corsets and restrictive undergarments were on the way out, so the new silhouette had to be achieved by other means.

Jean found she hit plateaus in her weight-loss trajectory every twenty-two to twenty-five pounds, but she didn't know if anyone else in her program was experiencing the same issues because discussion was not encouraged. She wondered if it was even worth it to stay at the clinic with that skinny Miss Jones and her seeming lack of empathy. "How could I follow someone who knew nothing about how fat people really felt? She'd never woken up in the middle of the night and eaten a cold pork chop between two pieces of three-day-old bread. She'd never popped a jellybean that she found in her son's blue jeans into her mouth, not minding that it was covered with crayon and lint." Talking was what Jean, forever the extrovert, craved—confessing her transgressions; admitting feeling guilty about cookies; celebrating victories, even if it was less than a pound lost; sharing her story so she knew she wasn't the only one trying to balance dieting with the pressures of a loving husband and young kids. She knew where to find her dieting compatriots—they were in class at the obesity clinic, surrounding her—but no one was allowed to talk. Finding another woman mourning the loss of her baby had helped Jean with that grief more than anything else.

During World War II, there was a shortage of mental-health therapists, and group therapy was used to help traumatized soldiers, not as a support method for dieters. In 1952, the annual American Medical Association conference held a session on "Weight Control—an Experiment in Group Therapy." It wasn't exactly a feel-good approach. *Time* magazine reported that "never before had the fat men & women of the U.S. received so much attention from doctors as they got last week at the annual meeting of the American Medical Association in Chicago. And none of it was flattering. Far from regarding the fatties as happy people, pleasant to have around, the doctors branded them as public-health problem No. 1 and cracked down hard on them. Said Philadelphia's Dr. Edward L. Bortz: 'We're going to have to take off the kid gloves in dealing with people who are wallowing in their own grease.'"

Talking was certainly encouraged at Overeaters Anonymous, which was so new—it was started in 1960 by a copywriter named Rozanne S.—that Jean might not have heard of it. (There was also an Eaters Anonymous, a Fatties Anonymous, and a Gluttons Anonymous.) OA was adapted from the twelve-step recovery program Alcoholics Anonymous, which was founded in 1940. "Obesity is the symptom most people identify with compulsive overeating," reads OA's handbook. "We know, too, how obese people have been patronized, prejudiced against, and exploited for economic gain. Charlatans and chicanery abound. Millions of dollars are made off the suffering of fat people, and this condition is probably the most prevalent health problem that exists in the American population." Their central question was: What do you need to recover? The answer: "Honestly admitting we were powerless over food...Compulsive overeating is a progressive illness."

The first national diet group, a kind of Weight Watchers precursor, was TOPS, for Take Off Pounds Sensibly; it was started in Milwaukee in 1948 by Esther Manz. Much like Jean, she was a wife and mother who felt she was addicted to food. At TOPS, once you reached your goal weight and maintained the loss for three months, you became a member of KOPS, Keep Off Pounds Sensibly. But the road to maintenance could be mortifying. A meeting might have a speaker and a forum for discussion, which sounds fairly standard. But weigh-ins were public. And if you gained weight, you had to stand in something called the pigpen wearing a prop like a bib along with all the other losers (well, gainers) from that week. Then you had to sing: "We are plump little pigs who ate too much fat, fat, fat / We are stout little pigs who can't resist food, food, food" to the tune of Yale's "Whiffenpoof Song." Another pigpen number was sung to the tune of "My Bonnie Lies Over the Ocean": "I am the Pig of my TOPS club / I am the cheater this week / I am the pig of my TOPS club—I've cheated and now I must squeak / Oink, oink, oink." In fact, music was quite central to TOPS. There was also "Lose, Lose," sung to the tune of "Skip to My Lou";

"You'll Be Petite-er," sung to the tune of "You Are My Sunshine" ("You'll be petite-er / And look much neater / If you select your food with care / Don't be a cheater, an overeater / The scales will tattle if you dare"). There was a song about drinking water set to the tune of "I've Been Working on the Railroad"; Christmas-themed songs ("'Tis the season of much snacking"); and a birthday song ("Happy birthday to you / May your gains all be few / Happy birthday, dear TOPS pal / Lose a clothes size or two"). If the pigpen penitentiary and songs of defeat weren't embarrassing enough, you also had to pay a fine that went into a piggy bank for gaining, and that week's biggest gainer was given a sign to put in her front yard that read I AM THE PIG OF MY TOPS CLUB. And yet, despite the enforced humiliation (or maybe because of it), the groups were so popular that within fifteen years of the organization's founding there were 60,000 TOPS members in local chapters with names like Shrinking Violets, Invisi-Belles, and Thick 'n' Tired. There are still chapters worldwide although they've modernized and done away with public weigh-ins and the pig song. Currently their website states, "Weekly meetings provide a supportive, educational environment where people are encouraged and not judged."

TOPS was silly and playful, and its members had a kind of esprit de corps; it showed that being fat didn't mean not having friends, and dieting didn't have to be an anonymous pursuit, all of which maybe fed a little off the idea that fat people were fundamentally lonely and sought food as solace. OA, on the other side of the spectrum, took a more ascetic path, with abstinence as the answer to overeating. Both relied on the strength-in-numbers approach, the centrality of confession, and the idea of surveillance, both by the self and the group. The group could be a stand-in for friends for the socially outcast fat person, but in TOPS there were competition and shame; in OA, confession and anonymity. What Jean wanted was something else. "All you need is one person in a group to be honest, and then slowly, very slowly, everyone else starts telling the truth."

On October 30, 1962, about a year after she'd started at the obesity clinic, Jean reached her goal weight of 142 pounds, a loss of 72 pounds, the exact weight Miss Jones at the clinic had assigned her. It had taken a year of hard work. "You want a miracle too, don't you? I know. We all want miracles. Unfortunately, it doesn't work that way," Jean said. "I've heard the complaints before. 'Takes too long.' 'I can't wait.' And I always tell people that the time is going to go by anyway— one way or another. You got to have a dream, and being slim is the dream in this case. Sometimes it's better not to focus too far ahead. Maybe all you're going to see that way is an uphill climb." She immediately gave away all her clothes except one dress, to serve as a reminder of her former self. She vowed never to touch chocolate marshmallow cookies again. Sometimes she'd let herself eat potatoes or an extra piece of bread or another kind of dessert, but Mallomars were like her size 44 dresses: never again.

"I took the *l* out of *flab*," Jean was fond of telling people. She celebrated with a makeover, buying, like Jackie Kennedy, shift dresses and fitted suits in chic shades of black and cream. She now wore a size 12, the equivalent of a modern size 6, and roughly the same dress size as Marilyn

Monroe. She didn't just want nice clothes, she craved them; she deserved them, now that they flattered her. "When I lost my weight, I felt like I was the one, that housewife who found the fountain of youth, and I wanted to give it to others," she said. She had just one more change to mark her new self: she wanted to be a blonde. (It wasn't an unusual fantasy; an advertisement of the era showed a woman declaring, "If I've only one life, let me live it as a blonde.") So Jean decided to dye her hair platinum, a shade she maintained until she died. She somehow managed to tie its maintenance to her weight loss. "It's not any more inconvenient to work on the size of you than it is to work on changing your hair color. I'm not thrilled about going for the touch ups, you know. I do it because I like the result." Jean's self-creation is reminiscent of Simone de Beauvoir's most quoted line from her pioneering book on gender, *The Second Sex*, which came out in 1949: "One is not born, but rather becomes, a woman."

Jean took to carrying a "before" picture with her at all times and liked to show off her own then-and-now success story. She had always been a leader, from vice president of her high-school class to the president of a local league for developmentally disabled children. "Whatever organization I got into, I usually ended up heading it," she said. She was filled with tips and advice and loved to share—maybe because she saw weight loss as a lifetime commitment and a struggle that, even though she was now thin, would never be over. There was no normal. "I pray that I never forget where I came from. I pray that I'll never get to the point where I'll think I've always been thin, successful, and at the end of the rainbow. I don't know of anybody who has been fat who ever feels totally safe again. We know we're not cured. We're merely arrested." Soon she started getting calls from strangers asking how she'd done it and if she could help them lose weight too.

CHAPTER SIX.

WHEN I FALL, I FALL HARD

September 2017

I had been keeping a running list in my journal of foods I missed and wanted, since I couldn't eat them, at least not in the quantity and frequency I would have liked. A good Weight Watcher would eat them in moderation, but what I missed was the self-immolating feeling of eating with no regard for calories consumed. So I didn't eat them at all and just wrote them down, as if that could be a satisfying substitute for Oreo Blizzards from Dairy Queen, Animal Style burgers from In-N-Out, fish and chips doused with malt vinegar. I missed french fries so much. Not just the extremely fancy kind fried in duck fat and served with steak in Paris—which I would have amputated a finger for—but even the frozen ones from the diner or lukewarm tater tots. Chocolate malted milkshakes topped with an extremely liberal amount of whipped cream. Fritto misto with fresh lemon juice squeezed over it, accompanied by a giant glass of white wine, eaten, hopefully, outside. Copious sushi orders. Cheese plates shared with friends. Giant round loaves of sourdough bread spread with salty butter. Turkey Reubens with a side of pickles and a root beer. Warm blueberry muffins with the nine-dollar raspberry cardamom jam I impulse-bought in Los Angeles. Lemon ricotta pancakes. A mountain of guacamole and tortilla chips and margaritas. To further torture myself, I followed three different accounts on Instagram that tracked news of junk food, as if just knowing that there was a new chili con queso or New England lobster roll flavor of Lay's chips would be enough to satisfy me.

It had been three months since I started the program, and I was feeling pretty virtuous about my dieting self, slightly thinner in my body, until I went to a Pilates class at a place on the Bowery in Manhattan. I liked this studio because it looked like the airy white loft of my dreams and stocked artisanal deodorant in the bathroom for you to freshen up with after class. It was also across the street from a Whole Foods and down the block from a French restaurant and I always spent a lot of time spacing out in class wondering what I should eat after.

In Pilates I caught a glimpse of myself in the mirrors that lined the side of the classroom. We were doing roll-downs on the reformer, sort of like a sit-up in reverse, and I was wearing a sports bra and leggings and was momentarily stunned by my belly fat overflowing between where my bra ended and the waistband began. How could I have so much of it? The *What's your why?* Weight Watchers devotees would have told me to let this keep me motivated, but instead, I let it darken my mood. I kept flashing back to it for the rest of the day.

(This happens all the time. I'll be just existing in my body and then I'm struck by a glimpse of what I actually look like and all that effort losing weight seems insurmountable.)

The previous week I'd gone to a movie with Vera. I didn't eat any of her Twix bars or buttery popcorn. The real compromise would have been to eat some reasonable amount, but I wasn't there yet. Instead, I spent the entire duration of the romantic comedy debating whether or not I should get a slice of pizza on the way home. If I hadn't been in the theater with a friend, I would have strongly considered leaving before the movie was over to go eat. Food shouldn't be so distracting that I ponder leaving a lauded Holly Hunter supporting role for it! I did get a slice of pizza, and the anticipation was far better than the payoff. That seems like the kind of sad food aphorism my mother would come up with, along with "A minute on your lips, forever on your hips," or something else out of a *Cathy* cartoon.

When I fall, I fall hard. A few nights after that, I got home at two a.m. from two birthday parties, which was an inordinately late hour for me, a person who often wakes up at five thirty in the morning of her own accord. I ordered a white pizza, partly because I was so impressed that I could do that in the middle of the night. I promptly fell asleep on my sofa and woke up to the sound of my buzzer at three a.m. I groggily accepted the pizza, ate more than half of it, retired to my bedroom, and ate the rest for breakfast. I ate it all quickly and without enjoying it much. (I eat everything quickly. I can remember twice at dinners when different friends have mentioned that I was eating more than my fair share of food, and I can't think of anything more mortifying.) Less than a week after the three a.m. pizza, I ate, over the course of three hours, a six-piece order of chicken strips from McDonald's, a McFlurry, half a carton of chicken lo mein, pork pot stickers, and three spare ribs.

I thought of a parable in *Yes You Can!,* a 1999 tome of advice from Rosalie Kaufman, who had been a Weight Watchers group leader for twenty-two years. She reported that a man told her, "Look at what a failure I am! I ate eight chocolate bars in a night!" And her response was "What I hear is you're counting." What is it about Weight Watchers leaders and their penchant for one-liners? Except I wanted to hide the evidence from everyone, even myself. The proper word would probably be *bingeing*—a word I abhorred so much, I wouldn't even use it to describe my TV-watching habits—or even *overeating,* but I thought of it instead as falling off the wagon. It felt less painful not to consider the activity very much. Sometimes I had paranoid fantasies that my group leader could access my Weight Watchers points in the app and see how poorly I sometimes did, so I did not even try to tally the points. Instead, I wrote in my food app, *I don't want to talk about it,* as if agents would be coming to my house to interrogate me. Maybe I was just talking to myself. I didn't know if there was an emotional trigger. That would have been the easy answer, but maybe I was bored of being good and wanted to misbehave in the way that I best knew how.

I love to eat. But do I love eating more or differently than a thin person does? I play so many games with myself. I used to have a rule that I could eat at McDonald's only at airports, but I travel so much for work that I felt guilty at how frequent that was, so I amended the rule: I had to be at an airport waiting for a flight departing the North American continent.

Maybe my outsize love of eating is why I've had trouble dropping the fork or resigning myself to a life of salads and skinless chicken breasts. I don't even know if I am willing to call my habits *compulsive*. They're certainly flawed, but I don't know if the problem is what I eat or how I eat it. And in the realm of coping mechanisms, is emotional eating so bad? I am so disconnected from my own hunger that I have never been able to tell when I'm hungry or what I want.

Food has always been synonymous with breaking the rules for me, first my parents' and now my own. I think of food in terms of moral value and order accordingly. Do I want to be good right now? Or am I being bad? Eating, for me, is really about transgression, a rebellion against myself. I've never understood it better than when I heard the psychotherapist Esther Perel talking about infidelity on a podcast. She said, "Something about breaking your own rules is intensely liberating. It makes you feel for the first time that you once again have a say, an agency over your life...not boxed in, even if it's a box that nobody is holding, it's just your own box."

I skipped meetings two weeks in a row because I didn't want to know how much I had gained. After that binge, or whatever I was refusing to call it, I ate a lot of salads to make up for it, and at the next meeting I went to, I'd lost three-tenths of a pound. That week's theme was "Make Your Meetings Matter." According to the company, members who attend meetings regularly are 11.2 times more likely to reach a 5 percent weight-loss goal at six months and

15.5 times more likely to reach a 10 percent weight loss at six months than those who attend fewer meetings are. The handout had answers to what marketing people might call "pain points"—that is, reasons for skipping a meeting. "My babysitter canceled" was paired with "Confirm 2 to 3 days ahead and have backup." "I feel like I've gained weight" had "Go to the meeting, find out for sure—and then make a new plan!" Going to meetings in person is about accountability, or maybe it's about interacting with people in person, even though Weight Watchers does have its own wildly positive social network whose enthusiastic tone is a little too high for my taste.

Or maybe meetings are really about humility. No one can see your weight, but knowing that you will be weighed and that it will be recorded is a motivating factor. I'd already found myself eating a light meal or purposely not making plans to eat out with friends the evening before a weigh-in. I worried that I'd get obsessive, that I'd start skipping meals and my eating disorder would take over. Or, less dangerous but still terrifying, that all this dieting would take over my life, that my personality would be replaced with a Stepford Diet version of me. I wanted to lose weight without losing myself.

Miriam talked about the importance of "finding a little bit of happiness in a journey that can feel fraught." Her message was that mind-set was important and maintaining a positive outlook would help us through the slog of weight loss. We were supposed to cultivate a healthy sense of well-being, but at the same time, we lived in a world where being fat was looked down upon, and those myriad stigmas affected well-being too. I was trying to right the wrongs of my past or course-correct, and in other ways, I was trying to give myself a better second half of my life. I wanted to make these choices for myself, not for my parents or because of the hangover of my upbringing.

Sometimes my whole interior life felt like a repetition of that pizza struggle while watching the Holly Hunter movie. A few days earlier, I'd wanted a burger, thought about it for an hour, still wanted it, and decided to order the burger, only to find out that my favorite place was closed. I ended up eating cereal, both lamenting the burger and feeling relief I hadn't eaten one. It never occurred to me to make the stir-fried jerk shrimp and peppers or Mexican scrambled egg sandwiches from recent Weight Watchers handouts or brave their social network for recipe ideas. My mother told me on the phone that her latest attempt to lose fifteen pounds included avoiding carbs to the point of picking out noodles from ramen. "It's unfair that I love food so much," she said and sighed so loudly I could hear her over the phone, 2,500 miles and three time zones away. I was ashamed food took up this much space in my brain, and yet, what way forward was there but to admit it?

The focus of Weight Watchers meetings seemed to be on variations of happiness; again and again, that's what people most commonly said they were chasing. But I wasn't sure if happiness was what I was after because, in a lot of ways, I was already there. If I had to name my superpower, it would be the ability to identify what I like and do more of it. I get a massage once a month; I swim laps on summer evenings when the city pool near my apartment is open; I go to horror movies. I didn't think losing weight would necessarily bring me happiness that wasn't already there. What I wanted was to remove the negativity and find peace, and those were different goals.

I was trying hard to love the meetings, even though I mostly took notes and nodded and smiled. I was no extrovert like Jean and I had a hard time chiming in when people were talking about their feelings. Maybe that was because I had my own friends and therapist to open up to. So much of Weight Watchers meetings is about being seen in the struggle (even if that meant, in my case, not saying much out loud), but it helps if you feel a connection to the people around you. I struggled with the same issues as my fellow Weight Watchers, but that was all we had in common. It was easier for me to talk to people I knew. Actually, that was a lie I told myself. What I really did was open up to almost no one and go around and around in my head.

Then again, in meetings that involved the nuts and bolts of losing weight rather than people's feelings, I got bored. I was committed to trying out Weight Watchers for a year but I was deeply ambivalent about dieting. I'd had a lifetime of extremely frustrating experiences, and it was hard to get over my skepticism that this attempt at losing weight would be any different. I also knew that not having a plan had led to me weighing this much. At the very least, Weight Watchers gave me a sense of control.

At the meeting, I stared at the people I was beginning to recognize as regulars: Patrice, the perimenopausal judge who had hovered fifteen pounds away from her goal weight for the past four months; Royce, the policeman who had high blood pressure and got winded too easily and was forty pounds down with sixty more to go; Rosemarie, the nurse who wanted to join the military; Sadie, the Orthodox Jewish mom trying to lose eighty pounds. I wondered if they were starting to recognize me, the woman who said nothing but smiled and made eye contact a lot and only wore workout clothes. I was so curious about their lives beyond these weekly meetings. I wondered if they skipped candy at the movies but were tempted by it the whole time, if they'd been fat since childhood, if their husbands or wives pressured them to join. I was torn between wanting to open up to everyone and wanting to just observe; between wanting to ask them all personal questions about why they were there and wanting to just give them space. My weight had been one of the hardest things in my life, and even though fat was written all over my body, I hated talking about it. I didn't want to ask them about it either. But if I didn't talk about this now, would I ever?

You can trace my life's trajectory through my weight. Or maybe through my eating habits. I first learned the power and transgressional pleasures of eating in college. I made a ritual of calling Pizza Time, which was about half a block away from my wood-paneled apartment, and having them deliver a medium pizza with ham and mushrooms. I never ate it at a table with friends. That pizza was all for me, blissfully alone by choice, sitting on the floor of my living room in front of the TV. And there was a diner I'd go to that served something called a Captain's Platter, which was a variety of fried seafood—shrimp, fish, maybe clams, all no doubt frozen—that came with french fries and coleslaw and some kind of buttery toast. Not that I ever told anyone about this habit back then. Food eaten surreptitiously became a way to distinguish my individuality from my parents'. Finally, they weren't there to control what I ate—something that, if they're around me to this day, they will still try to do—and I found a kind of endorphin rush from doing with abandon what I had been told my whole life was wrong. The thrill and the rush were compulsive and a little addictive, different from the elegant refusal of anorexia. Weight gain was a side effect and another kind of fuck-you to my parents, a way to reclaim control over my body. Or claim it—I'm not sure I ever had it in the first place. Subsisting on pints of Alaskan Amber beer and herbed bread rolls the size of my head from the school café was a welcome break from hypervigilance, but I weighed 170 pounds by the end of my sophomore year. If I weighed 170 now, I would consider celebrating in the streets.

During college I had a professor, a poet, who was probably 500 pounds and narcoleptic, so we had to have lectures in specific, accessible buildings because she couldn't walk upstairs very well. I hated her poetry and the fact that she would fall asleep and snore loudly while other people were talking and in other ways I thought she was bad at her job. But mostly, I hated how fat she was. Once when we were standing side by side at a deli on campus, I ordered a bagel with light cream cheese. "You don't need light cream cheese," she told me. I can't remember if I said anything, but in my head I was saying, *I do, or I'll be as big as you.*

Around the same time, I had my first serious relationship. I

wish I could say falling in love for the first time was some kind
of total healing experience for my body, but my boyfriend
was five eleven and weighed 135 pounds. I secretly wanted
to lose enough weight so that I would weigh less than him,
but in the seven years we were together it never happened;
instead, the gap between our weights just widened. He came
from the kind of family that had ludicrously balanced eating
habits. They ate salads with every meal, which they ate together, but also went out for ice cream or doughnuts a few
times a week.

He and I lived in Paris for a year. For my *carte de séjour*,
a kind of residence permit that went along with my student
visa, I had to visit a doctor in the suburbs just east of the
city. I had the short, requisite physical and sat opposite the
doctor's large desk waiting for him to sign my documents.
"Have you always been this fat?" he asked me in French. "Do
you eat a diet of foods rich in lipids?" When I'm shamed for
my weight, I freeze; my mind goes blank, and I have a kind
of out-of-body experience. This was over twenty years ago
and I don't have any kind of *esprit de l'escalier*—the French
phrase for thinking of a comeback after the fact—ready for
him even now. So I said no, I didn't think I ate a particularly
heavy diet and shrugged. Shrugging can let you get away
with a lot in France. He signed my papers. And I ended up
losing about thirty or forty pounds that year from jogging
laps around the moat of Château de Vincennes three times a
week. I didn't have a scale but I could fit into French clothes
sans problème.

I came home wearing head-to-toe black Agnès B. purchased
on my mother's credit card. She greeted me at the airport

in San Francisco and told me how thin I felt when she hugged me. That body didn't last. A diet heavy on burritos over my first year postgraduation had me topping the two-hundred-pound mark for the first time, officially obese. Soon after that, I attended a sold-out Belle and Sebastian concert and made my way toward the front to find a friend. Such a gentle band, it would be a place of meek and sweet people, right? Wrong. Two men standing behind me had a loud conversation comparing my body to a linebacker's. I was so sports-ignorant I had to look that up when I got home, but I could tell from the tone of their voices that it wasn't exactly a compliment.

I've been trapped in that cycle of gaining and losing the same pounds ever since, each time I lose plateauing at high and higher weights, and each time I gain creeping up on higher ones. Well into my mid-thirties I considered dieting my biggest secret. I wish I could say it was a thrilling one, like dating my college TA, but it's more like waxing my upper lip—I didn't ever want to talk about it, and I'd rather people thought I never had to worry about it in the first place. As the pounds would start coming off, I felt physically lighter. I slept well. I was in a better mood. But I also felt strangely furtive and isolated. A paranoia would creep in. The coded compliments, like "You look great," seemed to say so much about what people really thought of how I looked before. Once a personal trainer told me that I got back from vacation looking like I had given up on myself. And it's weird how many people there are willing to slap you in the face with their truth. I can achieve so much in life, and yet what stays with me are the comments about my looks. Eventually I'd drop vigilance for a day or two or a whole vacation, and suddenly my blouses would feel tight again. I hoped no one would notice and that I could just gain weight in plain sight, but apparently I couldn't hide it.

By the time I turned thirty-five, I was living in Brooklyn, going through a breakup, and diagnosed with clinical depression for the first time in my life. Food was the most reliable comfort I could find, cookie-dough breakfasts washed down with Diet Coke and the kind of delivery orders where the restaurant packs four sets of plastic utensils. I don't know if that's what I needed or what I wanted to be able to cope. The cocktail of pills I took—Lexapro, Abilify, Pristiq, Lamictal, Wellbutrin—helped lift me out of the dark fog, but they also elevated my weight. I hit 250, my highest ever.

The first time I saw a number that high on my own scale, my initial instinct was that I should die. Not commit suicide but disappear or turn into dust and evaporate. *Failure* isn't a strong enough word. Letting myself be fat hasn't ever felt to me like liberation. Activists say fat isn't something to be apologized for, but I've felt sorry about it my whole life. I believe I deserve equality and justice, but I'm not sure that the fight to demand it is any easier than the fight to earn it by losing weight. I believe that we all deserve space. If successful dieting requires living in my own body, I know that I'm just not always good at living in my own body.

I have never been able to comfortably live in whatever weight I am. Over the past five years I've tried six different meal-delivery programs and cheated on each of them. One of them involved so many salad greens that it turned my bowel movements dark green. At thirty-five I tried a medically supervised liquid diet, but if drinking two shakes as meal replacements and eating a sensible dinner à la SlimFast was easy to stick to, no one would be fat. At thirty-eight, I tried a different liquid diet and was so committed to it that, while reporting on a conference entirely dedicated to learning to stop dieting, I would duck into a bathroom stall during lunch and drink a high-protein shake, furtive as if I were going to do a line of coke. I once learned to program my computer just so it could block the food-delivery site Seamless but just ended up using it on my phone. In between the liquid diets, there was a doctor who devised a plan high in plant-based foods and protein. (And a few quirks—she had me eating two ounces of papaya every morning for digestion and milk with sugar at night. When I asked her if I could put honey instead of sugar in my milk, she replied, aghast, "Absolutely not.") After I weighed in with her each month, she'd say, in her thick Romanian accent, "You are going to look like model." When I was thirty-nine, a friend of mine told me about a doctor in a remote neighborhood in Brooklyn who would generously give anyone a prescription for Adderall. I made an appointment and then lost my nerve and canceled at the last minute. That same year I went on the antidepressant Wellbutrin because several of my friends had lost weight on it. (I didn't, and later its manufacturer, GlaxoSmithKline, was found guilty of criminal and civil liability "arising from the company's unlawful promotion of certain prescription drugs," according to the Department of Justice, and was fined $3 billion.) It's not a goal weight that I'm after (sometimes it's 130 or 150 or 170 or 190) but to lose enough weight that when I go to the Korean spa in Queens, the women working there won't automatically hand me the extra-large uniform that is somehow a totally different color than the rest of them. My parents are complicit in these schemes; they haven't paid for all of my efforts, but they have paid for the majority. I think I saw it as punishment and they seemed to think of it as a kind of reparation. We were all three holding on to the idea that I could just lose the weight and be done with it. But no one is ever done with it. That's the psychic burden we all feel about weight. Maybe what I should be asking myself is what kind of experience I want day to day. What kind of life do I want to give myself?

CHAPTER SEVEN

WHAT IS HER SECRET?

1962

Right away Jean saw flaws in the program at the New York City Department of Health, even while she was successful at it. She didn't like the way Miss Jones, the leader, dispensed information to the attendees. She suspected that her fellow members had their own stories about food but were too tied up in their own shame to share. Rather than dismiss her private quibbles with the program, Jean let herself imagine how it could be improved. Finding companionship and camaraderie was maybe even more important than the diet or even weight loss.

Ten weeks into her weight-loss program, Jean announced to her friends that she had lost twenty pounds. They wanted to know her secret. So she decided that she'd invite six of her friends who struggled with dieting to come to her apartment to play mah-jongg and she'd tell them what she had learned the day before in diet class. She wasn't yet at her goal weight, and she thought this would help her stick to the clinic's strict diet guidelines, and maybe her friends would lose some weight too.

The first meeting was a low-key affair. They settled in to play and chat. "They all have their secrets, their compulsive habits like mine that they kept to themselves," Jean said. But that afternoon they opened up to each other. Jean immediately felt that same liberation she had when talking to the woman in Florida who had, like her, lost a child. She looked around the room and realized that each woman was confessing about her habits and her life for the first time. Any initial embarrassment about what their friends might think of their favorite foods or midnight snacking turned to relief. Someone asked to meet again the following week, and Jean suggested they meet *every* week. That's how Jean the housewife created a space where a group of women struggling with their weight could come together and be honest about their lives. But it also gave Jean the spotlight she craved, a place to be funny and charismatic and glamorous, even if it was for an audience of a few friends. Years later she reflected back on those early meetings and said, without a trace of modesty, "It's as if, having never had a lesson, I sat down to a piano and played a concerto."

They called it Jean's Group and it grew quickly, going from six women to ten to forty within two months. And that was how it began. People would call and ask, "Can I bring my cousin?" "Can I bring my sister?" The answer was always "Sure, why not?" When Jean's chairs ran out, people would bring their own. Soon the group outgrew Jean's living room and spilled into her foyer, then they moved into her apartment complex's basement. She held meetings on both Wednesdays and Saturdays, and men even started coming. She was up-front with everyone, told them that she didn't have any background in science or nutrition, she was just a formerly fat housewife from Queens, as she liked to say. She taught people what she learned at the obesity clinic: avoid sweets and heavy foods and fill up on nutritious foods, never skipping meals. Alcohol and indulgent foods were a no, and liver was still mandatory. She didn't want people to try to lose six pounds in a week. Exercise wasn't her area of expertise or interest, so when asked about sagging skin or how to burn calories, she said that skin wasn't a problem if the weight was lost gradually and exercise was something to worry about when dieting was over. What was important to Jean was new eating habits. People would change into the lightest possible clothing, taking off jewelry and shoes, for the weigh-ins.

She wanted her friends to be as committed to being thin as she was. She didn't even think it was unrealistic to expect her followers to forgo dessert on holidays. "What is important is to be able to survive your own birthday party. To blow out the candles on your cake, serve it to your guests, and eat half a cantaloupe," she said. "Chances are you won't lose anything by giving up a slice of cake. But what you win is a big victory, and that can be the beginning of winning the war. I don't know if I even believed what I was saying, but it sounded good. I think I was just saying a lot of things that I knew were true but that I had avoided before—all my life, in fact, I had been sidestepping the truth about myself." She used terms like *survive* and *victory*. For her, weight loss and its maintenance was a kind of war with herself. But meetings were supposed to be an amusing oasis. Jean served coffee and encouraged laughter. As a meeting wrapped up, she would say, "If you leave here to have coffee and melon, coffee and fresh fruit cup, or coffee and friendship, I wish you well. But if you're leaving here to have coffee and a Danish, I affectionately wish you heartburn."

Jean had all manner of observations about the fat, none of which were very charitable. Having been fat and shed the weight, she thought she had earned the right to be harsh. "Thin people release the fork and they chew the food with the fork on the table. They chew their food slowly. They look around at each other or the wall or a picture. They listen to the music. They sit back and take a breath. They do something other than concentrate on shoving the food into their body," she said. "Overweight people never let go of their fork. They hold it when they are talking. They hold it when they are chewing. I discovered that is one of the secrets. Let go of the instrument that made you fat." When she received a letter from a ten-year-old girl asking what she could do about her weakness for bread, Jean asked her to think about how she felt after she had eaten her favorite bread. "Was it pleasure? If it was a pleasure, how long did it last? A minute? A few seconds?" she asked. "Think about the pleasure of being thin. Oh, it lasts so much longer and has so many other pleasures that go with it. Looking in the mirror and being happy with what you see. Putting on a dress that you like and look good in. Seeing a boy look at you with a smile, even if you don't care a pin about him. You can enjoy being a normal weight in so many ways all the time." She had plenty of sympathy for the plight of the fat—as long as they wanted to be thin.

Word got out that there was a woman in Queens who had lost weight. Was it fifty pounds? Was it a hundred pounds? It didn't matter because supposedly she was holding meetings to teach her friends how to diet. And thus Jean became a kind of traveling diet guru, taking her professional scale and sliding weights and throwing it all into her Studebaker to talk to any group that invited her. The thin bottle blonde would show up wearing something understated because she didn't want to distract anyone from what she was saying. She warned them that she wasn't one to mince words and would ask her audience why they made things so hard on themselves, if they'd rather waste food or waste themselves. She liked to call out members by name like a schoolmarm and ask them point-blank to describe their biggest food weakness. The newspaper columnist Jim Brady compared Jean to the Pied Piper, a nightclub entertainer, and a revival preacher.

In late 1962 she was invited to lecture at a couples club at the Long Island home of Albert and Felice Lippert. The two had married in 1953 and had young sons, Keith and Randy, around the same ages as Jean's children. Al was a buyer for a suit chain and he and Felice were social creatures. They liked entertaining, dancing, nights with their group of friends. They were the kind of parents who stressed a proper upbringing and manners for their kids but also told vivid stories at the dinner table about what had happened during the day. Felice and Al had also struggled with their weight, with Al calling them "two beach balls." Felice was tall and radiant; when she'd gone gray at the age of twenty, she made silver hair look elegant.

Jean came and talked to their group about herself, the foods they should and shouldn't eat, the importance of avoiding your Frankenstein, the food you could not control. As the evening was wrapping up, they invited her back the next week. By the next Friday get-together, Felice had lost four pounds and Al was down seven. So Jean kept coming back every week. The program worked: Al lost forty pounds and Felice almost fifty in four months.

The Lipperts thought that if Jean's program could help them, there was the potential to reach yet more people. They suggested turning her weight-loss salons into a proper business—franchising the idea and charging people a weekly fee to attend. Al knew what he could bring to the table; he was a marketer and could come on part-time, working behind the scenes on the business end with Felice while Jean continued to be the public face. Jean and Marty met weekly at the Lipperts' home for advice and it became a partnership, with Jean as president and treasurer, Marty as secretary.

What was missing was a name for this new business. Al suggested Jean go meet with his brother Harry Lippert, who was a lawyer, to make it official. He vetoed the name Jean's Group right away. "What if we call it Lose Pounds?" Jean asked. Harry said that was awful. "Watch Your Weight?" she tried. He thought that was even worse. "All right, what about Weight Watchers International?" said Jean. They didn't even have a single location yet but the international part was important to her—she had high hopes, and why not think big? "Mrs. Nidetch, that's ridiculous," Harry said. But he had all the papers signed and stamped and Jean was on her way. Weight Watchers International was incorporated in early May 1963.

That year, 1963, was pivotal. It was the year of Beatlemania, of the introduction of the Easy-Bake Oven and Tab diet soda. In early February, *The French Chef,* Julia Child's cooking show, began to air. Betty Friedan's *The Feminine Mystique* came out just eight days after Child's show premiered, on February 19. "The problem lay buried, unspoken, for many years in the minds of American women. It was a strange stirring, a sense of dissatisfaction, a yearning that women suffered in the middle of the twentieth century in the United States." That was how the Second Wave feminist classic on the drudgery of the housewife began. Jean was a much more typical housewife than Friedan, who'd had an academic career, or, for that matter, Julia Child, who had worked as a copywriter and in the Office of Strategic Services before championing French cuisine. Jean was also solidly lower middle class, the economic stratum where housewives were never truly just working in the home—they usually needed some other job to help sustain the family. Jean was familiar with the dissatisfaction of living a purely domestic life. She had never been successful at simply cooking and cleaning for Marty and the boys—whether she was styling women in Tulsa or selling eggs door-to-door in New York City, she always ended up working. As Friedan wrote, "Each suburban wife struggled with it alone. As she made the beds, shopped for groceries, matched slipcover material, ate peanut butter sandwiches with her children, chauffeured Cub Scouts and Brownies, lay beside her husband at night—she was afraid to ask even of herself the silent question—'Is this all?'"

Julia Child, Betty Friedan, and Jean Nidetch weren't answering the same societal questions, they weren't all avowed members of the women's movement, and they may not have all voted for the same political party, but they were working in a kind of tandem to tackle the problem of women needing an outlet for expressing themselves. Child was addressing the American midcentury pharmaceutical way of thinking about food and holding up the French as an antidote by encouraging the enjoyment of the simple pleasures of cooking, with liberal use of butter. Friedan was pointing out the flaws in the 1950s domestic paradigm, that femininity and pleasing one's spouse and children were never going to be everything to a woman, nor should they be. Ostensibly, Weight Watchers was about dieting, which was in line with the feminine confines Friedan vilified, and it embraced artificial sweeteners and butter substitutes and a culture of restriction that Child worked against, but at its core, Jean's organization was about strength in numbers and giving women a place to listen to and support each other. Jean's idea was for women to come together and talk about their issues with food, which was really talking about the reality of their lives.

Weight Watchers still didn't even have an office. Jean wanted to find a public place to hold meetings that would save her from the endless commuting of the previous year. She found a little loft space on the second floor above a movie theater in Little Neck, Queens, that she rented for $75 per month. She decided they'd charge $2 for a meeting, the same as the tickets to the theater. She needed the money—her bank account had a balance of $1.56; she later had the statement framed. Jean had the genius to see both what was ineffective in her Department of Health program *and* to fashion a solution. She wasn't afraid to charge money to help people lose weight. Jean was poised to start her own empire, but she still had to go home to Marty first. She couldn't get the lease without her husband's signature.

CHAPTER EIGHT

WHAT DOES BEING THIN EVEN MEAN?

October 2017

I was writing a story for *Vogue* that entailed trying out a number of expensive bodyworkers who had cult followings of models and actors and dancers for their ability to drain the body of bloat through (extremely painful and often bruising) lymphatic massage. I left a combination scrub-infrared wrap-lymphatic massage feeling less puffy than I'd felt in a long time, my stomach as flat as if I'd just gotten over a stomach flu. I put on my billowy pants and a linen T-shirt and made my way back through the lobby, where I saw *Top Chef* host and former model Padma Lakshmi in the waiting area. I stared at her for a few seconds too long, but I didn't have to wonder what she was doing there—the same Brazilian woman who had just kneaded me for an hour came out and hugged her. Lakshmi didn't seem to be subjected to the same elements that I was. She was wearing stiletto boots and a leather jacket despite the eighty-degree Indian summer humidity outside. Instantly I was brought down to earth. I felt dumpy again.

Dieting and the desire to change or refine your body are not solely the domain of fat people. The beautiful people I so often encounter in my job go to extreme lengths to maintain their bodies. I have begun to see thin as its own class—people who maintain their weight as part of their lifestyle. There's the class we are born into and the class we strive to belong to. To what lengths will we go to earn our class position? How much do we fear falling from it?

I had been exercising a lot too, not out of duty but because I was beginning to love it. I was a late bloomer in terms of falling for exercise, learning how good it could feel to just move and stretch. Exercise as a kid was a punishment for me, like dieting, but I'd surprised myself with my ability to make peace with it. I wish I could stick to any diet as much as I can stick to exercising a few times a week. I wish I were able to look at dieting that way. Maybe I just need to own the fact that every other relationship is easier than the one I have with food. With the exception of the time I booked a SoulCycle bike right next to a mirror, exercising makes me feel more connected to my body, which feels stronger, more flexible, and also, yes, a bit smaller and more muscular. It's time out of my head to just live in my body. I love that everyone is sweating and struggling together—another moment where I realize the body struggle is truly universal. Early one Sunday morning at a SoulCycle location in Brooklyn, I was, as usual, one of the fattest people in the room. But I realized that all these people were not selling out a class because they simply loved being awake and exercising at eight a.m. on a Sunday but rather because they were trying to manage the same struggle to feel healthy and look good that I was. Even when Jean was thin, she never stopped talking about the effort involved in maintenance. Nothing is ever as easy as it appears.

I read an article about a football player who was ridiculed for being fat. He was six feet tall, and at his heaviest, he was 267 pounds; he'd since lost around twenty pounds. I weigh more than him now. I'm jealous of him. I'm jealous of everyone, really. I constantly compare myself to friends, to women in yoga class, to plus-size models on Instagram. More than once, I've found myself jealous of my bulldog. Once I was walking her at night and heard someone yell out, "She's so chubby!" I felt a wave of shame that someone was screaming about my body on the street, which has happened many times before. (On a holiday trip to Paris a few years ago, two different strangers called me fat. Both times I was walking down the street in an oversize motorcycle jacket and skinny jeans when I was called out for being "a *beeg* girl.") Then I saw two teenage girls running over to coo at Joan and realized they were praising her chubbiness. I was tempted to correct them and tell them she was actually in great shape, just had a lot of loose skin, but I stopped myself. We all just accept dogs for showing up. I wish I could do that for myself.

There's a game I play where I scan every room to see if I'm the fattest person there—I think a lot of women probably engage in some form of this cruel routine—and almost always confirm that I am. Last winter I attended an invite-only yoga retreat in Miami that included not one but two Brazilian models, an actress from a hit television show, a social media star, a lifestyle guru, two fashion designers, and a celebrated fashion photographer. Plus their boyfriends, almost all of whom had man buns. I walked out to a rooftop yoga class the first day and realized I was at least seventy-five pounds heavier than any of the other women and some of the men.

The role I take on for my job is that of a thoroughly believable Everywoman. I'm also the person editors call on to profile celebrities like Jennifer Hudson, Chrissy Metz, and Roxane Gay for frank interviews about their own attempts to lose weight. I can ask famous women how much they currently weigh or if they have been mistaken for being pregnant because I can tell them about my own struggle. Or maybe I don't have to tell them; they can see it in my body. It would be much harder for a thin woman to ask those kinds of questions. I have sat for meals with the numerous models I have profiled—Karlie Kloss, Helena Christensen, Joan Smalls, Stella Maxwell, Imaan Hammam—and they almost always explain to me that they are keto, or paleo, or gluten-free, or quit sugar *for their health*. (I don't believe most models when they tell me it's all about balance, with the exception of Christie Brinkley, who I interviewed while she ate an entire pizza. It was a personal-size, but I was still impressed.) I'm always wondering what these women think of my body, if they are jealous because they think I've given myself license to eat with abandon or if they'd rather be dead than be my size. Sometimes I think my size is an asset to my job, that it's easier for the most beautiful and famous women to relax and open up to someone they don't perceive as a threat. I've also come away with a greater sense of humanity; I have watched these women pick at their quinoa salads as they bare their insecurities to me. I know firsthand that food and weight are things that take over a significant portion of their lives too. The actress Zosia Mamet once told me over a breakfast interview (I had a bagel and lox; she had an almond-milk latte), "It's an endless roller coaster of that tiny voice and it's always present."

When I was twenty-six, my first glossy magazine feature was accepted. Imagine my delight when the editor in chief, a protégée of none other than Anna Wintour, wanted to feature an interview with me in the Contributors section. There had to be an accompanying photo, though, so I excitedly sent along a selection that I thought made me look smart, stylish, and a little edgy. The editrix swiftly nixed them all. Her decision was relayed in polite, impersonal tones by an assistant. But I knew what the real message was: I was too fat to grace the pages of the magazine. They ended up using a "flashback" photo of me at age sixteen, lithe but anorexic. When it was published, a friend who hadn't known me as a teenager, a former model herself, said she and her husband saw the photo and thought I looked better now, "on the fuller side." Instead of being angry at all of it, I felt like it was what I deserved.

I spent a weekend in Montauk with Jennifer, one of my best friends. I've known her since we went to college together, and we moved to New York a year apart. She is one of the only friends I talk to about weight because she struggles too. During our first semester, she and I used to buy candy corn and then, immediately after opening the bag, dump most of it out the window of our dorm room so it wouldn't be there to tempt us—out of sight, out of mind—until Campus Safety knocked on the door and asked why there was a mound of candy corn outside her window. Apparently, the grounds crew had complained. Just because you can't see it doesn't mean it's gone away.

She's always been a little smaller than me, probably only a size 12, which I envy even more than the fact that she owns an apartment with a washer and dryer. Her job in the costume department at the ballet exacerbates her feelings about her body the way interviewing celebrities does my own. Or maybe I can talk to her about it because she's known me for twenty years and has seen me at every weight between 150 and 250 pounds. She recently found a photo of the two of us taken in 1997 in an alley in Seattle. I look at myself and think I look the same, but maybe that's not true? I was sixty or seventy pounds lighter then, maybe more, but I vividly remember feeling so fat. Now I look at the picture and I think my body was normal and even cute. I wish I'd known how to stop fighting the self-hatred then, or to try to maintain my weight, or not to feel like a failure. If I thought I was a failure then, what am I now? How much time have I lost to hating the way I look?

Jennifer was doing Weight Watchers from home and I thought I might be the only person who knew. She certainly didn't tell her on-again web designer boyfriend who played drums in a psychedelic rock band. He once told me he loved her thunder thighs, which made me instantly hate him. "I would never set foot in a meeting. You couldn't pay me," she'd said. I didn't know how much she'd lost or how much she wanted to lose. My guess would be that she'd lost ten, maybe fifteen pounds and wanted to lose twenty-five more. She'd joked that she'd lost a hundred pounds over the course of her lifetime, but it seemed too intrusive or not supportive to ask her, some kind of unspoken boundary in our friendship. I had for so long dieted and eaten in secret that even speaking candidly with Jennifer about dieting and the body was difficult, although she too was on the program. It was a little sad that the one friend I considered myself having an open dialogue with about my body was someone I still enforced a barrier with. Part of what's always made dieting so torturous for me is that I feel like there's almost no one I can really be honest about it with. Weight can intrude on our core relationships.

In Montauk we ate well and healthily—omelets with greens and fruit, and we split scallops, pasta, salad for dinner. We laughed at our attempts to estimate how many tablespoons of butter and oil were in our food in order to log the points. I didn't eat a single piece of candy from the minibar.

I'm astounded at how much effort it takes for me to make good choices. I constantly feel like I deserve a reward for eating well. If it's not going to be an ice cream sundae, what is it going to be? If I've decided it's no longer going to be eating a bowl of pesto pasta the size of my head, I don't know what it is. What I want is a new kind of bad, a way to rebel against myself that doesn't involve food, to disengage food from morality. Weight Watchers would probably tell me to make a low-points version of pesto thinned with broth and serve it over zucchini noodles (a dish that graces the cover of a booklet entitled "Eat Better" that I was given when I signed up) and enjoy myself. But I know that healthy compromises just don't entirely do it for me; there's still a pleasure center somewhere within that wants some oblivion. When I've done strict diets in the past, my eating was replaced by shopping. Substituting one vice for another feels like playing that arcade game Whac-A-Mole, the one where the plastic moles pop up from their holes and you have to use the mallet to try to flatten them.

After almost four months of meetings, I weighed in and found I was down eight pounds. It wasn't nothing, but it also wasn't a lot. The meeting's discussion topic was "Stand Up to Stigma." Weight Watchers suggested moving items in the category of "Unhelpful Thoughts" (such as "I don't blame the flight attendant for rolling her eyes when I asked her for a seat-belt extender") to "Reality Check" ("If my friend thought this, I would tell her she did not deserve to be treated like that") and, finally, to "Rethink It" ("I'd ask the flight attendant for a pillow or blanket. I shouldn't feel bad about asking her for a seat-belt extender"). I liked that Weight Watchers looked at weight's stigma, but I wished they would go further than seeing it as a problem between you and another individual and see it as a problem that can really only be solved by societal change. Then again, Weight Watchers was a diet company. I had to remind myself of that fact a lot.

The stereotype was that the meetings were just a bunch of fat people sitting around talking about how much they hated themselves and how they wanted to look like some unattainable ideal, but I did credit Weight Watchers for bringing together several dozen people to talk about topics like insecurity and struggle at nine a.m. on a Sunday.

"Coming here gives me relief because Weight Watchers gives me tools to deal with the stigma of my weight," Patrice the judge said. "We carry a stigma for ourselves. If we say it doesn't matter, then we don't care about ourselves." I'd noticed she was an especially active listener, nodding and laughing and wrinkling her face at whatever people in the room said. I wondered if she was like that in the courtroom. I had a momentary fantasy of getting called for jury duty and asking to recuse myself because the judge and I went to the same diet center.

Royce brought a body experience of his own, about the bulletproof vest he wore in the police force. "I wear a vest and it's almost like a girdle," he said. "For women, they make them specific, but they don't make a fat-person vest. There were many nights I wouldn't wear them. Now that I've lost sixty-five pounds—the vest is still hot and sweaty and slightly uncomfortable, but it's not to the point I can't wear it." We clapped. "People keep asking me, Are you okay? Because I look so much thinner," he said. He had about forty more pounds he wanted to lose. "I eat all day long, but I'm just munching on fruits and vegetables. A couple guys at the station joined because I was losing so much and now another guy and me, we have conversations all day about points."

I felt a twinge of self-consciousness for having pegged the officer as a meat-and-potatoes kind of guy. Part of what interests me about Weight Watchers is its popularity and ability to bring people together from all walks of life. There is so much talk of living in our political and cultural and socioeconomic bubbles these days, and I'm in no way an exception. I was raised in a family that was critical of the criminal justice system in America—my father is a criminal defense attorney. Learning about the intimate feelings a police officer had about his own body and the vest that he wore was new for me. My friends mostly work in creative fields or are fellow writers and live different lives, for the most part, than the people in this group. I know so few people in my own small circle who struggle with weight or, at least, talk about it. Instead of trying to project beliefs and lives on these people I met in meetings, I wanted to just take them for who they were and see what we had in common as people. And yet, sharing a struggle wasn't quite enough to make a commonality. I wondered if in Jean's time, she just had more in common with the other ladies of Queens who, like her, were trying to lose the weight. While I had weight in common with my fellow Weight Watchers, I wasn't sure that held my interest enough. Weight Watchers didn't offer me much in the way of sensual, intellectual, or cultural pleasures. Which is not to say I'm so effete that I need to be stimulated by every pursuit but that, taken on its own, dieting is just really boring by nature.

What does being thin even mean for a person? Healthy living is a symbol of wealth; dieting is a way to show off how much disposable income you have. People with more money have the resources to eat well and the luxury of being able to pay a lot of attention to their habits. Fresh fruits and vegetables and whole grains and lean meats shouldn't be expensive, but they are, as are the trendy supplements and powders and gluten replacements and heritage produce that we think we need to lose weight. So by having a fat body, I am a class traitor because I am visibly squandering the advantages of my upbringing—I have both the knowledge and the access, yet I still can't manage to successfully keep weight off.

My fantasy for my body is to be whatever size it is and for no one to see me as fat; for the social perception of fatness to cease to exist. I think it's less about a hatred of fat people or my body and more about wanting to be able to live in a way where I am noticed for what *I* choose. That represents an ease in society, one whose worth can't be underestimated. Then again, how many people get to dictate how the world sees them? Maybe fat people are just made more aware of the negative ways that the world views them because fat shaming is very acceptable in our culture. And fat is visible. In this era of total body vigilance, is there any kind of middle ground where one is neither too fat nor shockingly thin?

I'm using health and being thin interchangeably, but that's not entirely the case. There seems to be no definitive answer on whether fat is inherently bad for my health or neutral, or if quitting dieting would do more good to my mental health than harm to my body. According to the National Institute of Diabetes and Digestive and Kidney Diseases, 70 percent of American adults are overweight or, like me, obese. Obesity is linked to all manner of health problems by the Centers for Disease Control, including high blood pressure; high LDL cholesterol, low HDL cholesterol, and high levels of triglycerides; heart disease; type 2 diabetes; sleep apnea; stroke; gallbladder disease; osteoarthritis; and endometrial, breast, colon, kidney, gallbladder, and liver cancers. In addition there are more diffuse conditions, such as clinical depression, "body pain and difficulty with physical functioning," "low quality of life," and "all causes of death (mortality)." Weight isn't even a cut-and-dried risk factor for everyone; some people are affected extremely adversely by weight gain, and others are not. Even if one is fat, there's still the matter of the kind of fatty tissue one has. The nefarious-sounding *visceral fat* lies deeper under the skin and surrounds the organs and can impair their function, and it's mostly found around the abdomen. People who are apple-shaped, like me, are considered to be worse off than people who are pear-shaped because we gain weight in the abdomen and have more visceral fat.

The nation's obesity crisis isn't due solely to the fact that America is growing fatter. What is considered overweight has changed over the years. BMI is used to calculate healthy weight ranges by height—you take your weight in kilograms and divide it by your height in meters squared. At a BMI of 25, you are overweight; over 30 is obese. A person with a BMI above 40 is considered extremely obese, and more Americans live with that diagnosis than HIV, Parkinson's disease, Alzheimer's, and breast cancer combined. But the very idea that there are standardized ranges that determine health is itself flawed. Bodybuilders, for example, have high BMIs despite being very lean because they have so much muscle and therefore relatively high body weights. And certainly there are plenty of people with BMIs in the normal range who are staying there via unhealthy measures. BMI is most effectively used to look at trends in large populations but it has become the easy gold standard in judging weight-related health. But other measures for looking at health include blood pressure and cholesterol, glucose levels after fasting, and inflammation.

In 1997, the World Health Organization issued a report that called the rise in obesity an epidemic. One of the effects was that, in 1998, the National Institutes of Health lowered the threshold for what was considered overweight, going from a BMI of 27 for women and 28 for men to anyone with a BMI over 25. The author of the WHO report, Philip James, stated, "The death rates went up in America at 25 and they went up in Britain at 25 and it all fits the idea that BMI 25 is the reasonable pragmatic cut-off point across the world. So we changed global policy on obesity." This must have come as a shock to millions of people who, overnight and with no change in their body size, went from being considered normal to being overweight and therefore unhealthy. Something like the umbrella term *prediabetes,* for glucose levels that lie above normal but below that defined for diabetes, has been thrown around for the past fifteen years or so, but some doctors have criticized this new diagnosis as unnecessary.

Forty-five percent of Americans worry about their weight all or some of the time, which shows a significant increase from the 34 percent in 1990 who reported that they worried to that extent. And a 2008 study found that half of three- to six-year-old girls worry about being fat. The psychological effects of being fat are hard to quantify and understudied, but we do know that in health care, weight bias is dangerous. Anyone who is fat has stories of going to the doctor for something completely unrelated to weight, say, an ear infection, and getting a lecture on losing weight. I broke my ankle and my orthopedist, a fat man himself, said that crutches would be hard for me to navigate with because "you're no skinny little thing." I had an appointment with a doctor to get a referral for a mammogram; she gave it to me but not before she told me I should lose a hundred pounds and advised me to go to Costco to buy weight-loss tea. Studies have found that doctors are failing their obese patients due to their own prejudice against fat people, finding them more annoying and a waste of their time. Research has shown that doctors fail to refer obese patients for proper diagnostic tests and spend less time with them. The result is that a lot of fat people are underserved by the medical system and they, in turn, avoid doctors altogether.

I understand that doctors are sometimes required to tell overweight patients about the risks of obesity, but one major problem is that they don't have great solutions. People who are fat know they're fat, and they know the solution is some combination of eating less and moving more. But it is not that easy. When you lose weight, physiological adaptations occur to reduce the number of calories the body burns, so you have to cut more and more calories to keep losing weight. Your brain makes you crave sweets or fatty or salty foods and your body feels less full. Basically, your body and your brain are working together to prevent you from losing weight as a defense against starvation. My body would do great in a hunger winter, but instead I live in New York City, surrounded by bagels and artisanal ice cream. Diets so often fail because they are too strict, too focused on the short term, and our goals are too untenable. Statistically speaking, diets don't work very well, especially in the long run. In a 2007 meta-analysis of thirty-one long-term diet studies, researchers at the University of California, Los Angeles, found that one-third to two-thirds of dieters gained more weight within four or five years than they'd initially lost. Syracuse University journalism professor Harriet Brown, author of *Body of Truth: How Science, History, and Culture Drive Our Obsession with Weight—and What We Can Do About It*, believes success is even rarer than that: "Dieting doesn't make people thinner or healthier unless you're one of the 3 to 5 percent whom it can work for in the long term," Brown says, using an estimate based on the hundreds of men and women she interviewed for her book, only a handful of whom had lost more than twenty pounds and kept the weight off.

I remember reading about people who successfully keep weight off, a feat so hard that it merited a long article in the *New York Times Magazine*. The story described one of the women measuring her small serving of Ben and Jerry's ice cream. A lifetime of measuring sounds like hell to me. It's not how I want to live. But when I lose weight, I think I've become a thin person. I don't have that constant vigilance in me. I am not sure I even want it. But to be thin, I would probably have to resign myself to a lifetime of calorie-counting and strict exercise regimens. Dieters like me have lost weight. I can white-knuckle my way to losing twenty pounds, forty pounds, eighty pounds again and again, but keeping the weight off has somehow proved to be an even greater challenge than losing it. This pattern could be detrimental to more than my resolve; the American Heart Association published a preliminary study in 2019 that found that yo-yo dieting might increase the risk of heart disease.

We should be less concerned with thinness as the indicator of health. Just think of thin children who play video games all day and eat junk food. A better approach would be to focus on behavior change for everyone. Not just the basics we hear about endlessly, like fresh produce and lean meat and whole grains and cooking your own food, but on consistency. That doesn't mean eating the kinds of regimented daily meals starlets like to list in women's magazines (breakfast: oatmeal; snack: six almonds; lunch: a large salad; dinner: fish and vegetables) but rather having a nutritional consistency and balance in the food we eat. The problem comes when I try to apply this to myself.

CHAPTER NINE

THE MESSAGE IS, I'M ONE OF YOU

1963

Four hundred people came to the first Weight Watchers meeting in Queens on May 15, 1963, a crowd that shocked Jean. They had only fifty chairs, so they sent the overflow out to kill time until the next meeting; these people probably went to eat one last pastry before they started their diets. Jean was nervous, which was a rare emotion for her, but she looked out at the gathered people and realized she didn't even know many of them. They were strangers who looked just as dejected as she had been a year and a half before. Now they were looking to her for the same hope she had been looking for. Weight Watchers had successfully tapped into a collective anxiety of getting fat, and now that there were more people who were considered overweight and, in turn, who considered themselves overweight, they all wanted to take action.

Jean sat on a table on a platform at one end of the room

and called the meeting to order with a gavel. Happy to tell her story, and in an attempt to exert some control over the room, she started talking about herself. She was delighted to find that people listened. She asked if some of them ever got panicked over their size, if they couldn't turn around in the confines of a phone booth or climb out of a two-door car. "What hurt you? You don't have to share it with anybody but when you're alone, looking at cookies, I want you to remember what hurt you," Jean said, looking around the room. The primary question was whether they really *wanted* to lose weight. Somewhere along the line in life, someone had said that they couldn't do it, it wouldn't work. "Feeling in charge of yourself, the feeling that you've made it in the struggle, that I-Can-Do-It feeling," does spread into other parts of your life, she said. "I've seen it over and over and over in work, in love, in relationships. I call it dignity."

People started to contribute their own stories. A woman said that she went on vacation and gained weight. "What happened, did you eat the hotel?" Jean asked. Usually the truth came out as guilty confessions. In an early meeting a guy said he would stop by a doughnut shop and eat a dozen doughnuts in his car. A woman stood up and said, "That's nothing. I once stopped at a roadside hot dog stand. A guy says to me, 'How many?' Out of me comes, Four. I got four hot dogs, four hamburgers, four bags of french fries." No one was shocked at this story and nobody laughed. Jean never said it was ridiculous. She might poke fun but she had heard and eaten it all herself.

Another day the group was talking about their particular food passions, the topic closest to Jean's Mallomar-loving heart. These were great years for worshippers of sweet treats and savory snacks; in a two-year span in the mid-1960s, Pop Tarts, Cool Whip, and Doritos all hit stores. But during that meeting, one woman said she just couldn't think of anything in particular. The group moved on to other subjects. Then, right in the middle of the session, came a wail from the back of the room. "Pumpernickel!" It was that woman, enunciating each syllable. "You know why? It's my husband's fault. He works late and he brings home hot pumpernickel bread." Jean looked her up and down. Pumpernickel bread on its own didn't seem to be the offender. "Do you eat it dry?" she asked. "No. I put cream cheese mixed with walnuts on it." Okay, Jean said, thinking she was on to something. "Do you ever eat just nuts?" "Oh, I love nuts," the woman replied. "Where do you keep them?" "In the oven," the woman responded. "So the kids won't find them." And that's when Jean nodded—she had finally gotten to the truth. "It's nuts," she said. "Who can eat just one nut? I told her it's better not to eat any." Her other advice was to wash your cookies like fruit. "But they won't taste the same," someone would always protest. "That's the point," Jean would say. This was something Jean herself practiced. She no longer needed to tell the boys at the deli because they always remembered to wash her coleslaw so she could have it on her turkey sandwiches. Or she'd tell everyone to go home and gather up those potato chips or quarts of strawberry ice cream and take them out of the wrappers and really mash them into the garbage so it was gooey and smelly. Or hold them under the water faucet and watch them dissolve into nothing. "Down the drain and not down me," Jean trilled. "How do problem foods get in your home? Do they float in? You have a magician for an enemy who likes to torment you?"

One of her favorite anecdotes was about how she stayed a bottle blonde. She loved brunettes, didn't think there was anything wrong with them, it's just that she didn't want to be one. It was the same with being someone who put on weight naturally but who had to work very hard to keep it off. "Every three weeks I spend three hours in a beauty shop. It's not any more convenient to work on the size of you than changing your hair color. Let your good, healthy vanity express itself!" Vanity was a good thing for Jean, as was constant vigilance. "One lapse leads to another. A person who consistently passes a red light gets careless. When you feel tempted to slip, do it in the presence of another human being. Look in the mirror, think of what you know about you and what you want to be. Really see yourself and ask yourself if it's really worth the price," she said.

Jean would show up in high heels with her hair always done, a fresh manicure and pedicure. She told her staff that they too were to look like impeccable "after" photos, to look the part of someone who had dramatically changed. "Be elegant but never above the fray," she said. "The message is, I'm one of you." Jean was possessed of an almost mythical relatability among her followers. She was just a fat housewife who got thin and wanted to talk about it.

She wasn't the sole diet guru in an era where dieting was for the first time becoming an entrenched part of the culture. Dr. Robert Atkins was an attractive young cardiologist from the Upper East Side of Manhattan who, like Jean, lost weight and adapted his own version of the ultra-low-carb diet by Dr. Alfred W. Pennington. Also like Jean, Atkins was fond of a sweeping pronouncement. He wrote in *Dr. Atkins' Diet Revolution*, "Martin Luther King had a dream. I, too, have one. I dream of a world where no one has to diet." Jean appeared alongside him on television several times over the years. "I never argued with him. I'm not out to put down anybody else's weight-loss diet," she said. She just thought that a sound program for losing weight had to have three vital components: it had to provide a plan for better health, it had to be something you could stick to for the rest of your life, and it had to be able to travel. "In any town, any home, any restaurant," Jean would say, but liked to add with a sly little smile that at Weight Watchers, you didn't have to be afraid of carbs. Nathan Pritikin's 1974 book, *Live Longer Now*, was all the rage with West Coast bohemians who adopted the ultra-low-fat, low-protein diet that required followers to eat 80 percent of their food in complex carbs; it had begun as a treatment for heart-disease patients in his spa-like Santa Barbara clinic. Pritikin and Atkins sometimes appeared in the media together as diet foils and never had a kind word for each other. Pritikin said that the Atkins Diet could cause constipation, bad breath, heart disease, and cancer, and in turn Atkins threatened to sue him. There was Harold Katz, who started the diet program Nutrisystem, which provided its own food and touted "good" carbs, high fiber, and protein (for example, cookies made from oats) and made so much money that Katz bought the Philadelphia 76ers basketball team. By the mid-1960s, bariatrics, the treatment of obesity, had become a medical subspecialty, and by 1972 there were

450 members of the American Society of Bariatric Physicians (in 2015 the group changed its name to the Obesity Medicine Association).

Jean personally taught three classes a day in Little Neck. Loyalty to her was fierce. A group of women from Providence, Rhode Island, traveled in together each week for class. When there was a blackout, class was conducted by candlelight. The success stories started coming too. One woman said she was no longer embarrassed to be seen picking her son up from school. Someone else celebrated finally being able to cross her legs.

Florine Mark came all the way from Detroit for the program. She was just under five feet tall and weighed 165 pounds. Mark grew up poor, living with thirteen relatives under one roof, and earned the nickname Fat Flo (a play on *fatso*), which was then shortened to FF. When she complained about it to her mother, she'd tell Mark to sit down and have a piece of cake, that then she'd feel better. She tried speed, thyroid pills, and something called the ice cream diet and had lost fifty pounds and gained it back at least nine times before she heard about Jean. She was in her late twenties and had given birth to five children in seven years. Her husband said she should start thinking about going to work, but she didn't think anyone would hire her because she was so fat.

In a magazine, she saw a story about Jean. She found her number and called up Weight Watchers and asked for Mrs. Nidetch. "I'm here in Detroit and I need to lose weight. Can you send me the diet?" she asked. "I can't do that, you have to go to class," Jean said, but eventually she agreed. Mark ended up sending Weight Watchers ten dollars and trying it on her own. She hated how strict it was. You couldn't have watermelon and you couldn't have mayonnaise. She didn't get how it could work. So her parents came to stay with her five kids so she could go to New York City and make a pilgrimage to an actual Weight Watchers meeting. She could hardly make it up the stairs to the Little Neck location. But once she got to the meeting, she was enchanted by Jean— tall, beautiful, with an earthy charisma. "She spoke from her heart," Mark said. "I must have heard her tell her story at least a hundred and fifty times, and every time she brought me to tears and brought me to laughter. She had a gift and I don't hear speakers like that." Jean had her recommit to the diet. "You will eat liver once a week, you will eat fish, and you have no choice," she said. Mark stayed for five days, attending three classes a day and taking the subway to Weight Watchers from a seedy hotel on Queens Boulevard where she'd open the drapes onto a view of cement. On the fifth day, she got weighed. She was convinced that she had gained weight, but was thrilled to see she had lost five and a half pounds. She kissed Jean, who sent her home to Detroit, where she ended up losing forty pounds in four months. She felt energetic, even with five young kids running around, and she had a sense of accomplishment and self-respect she hadn't thought was in her.

What Mark learned for herself was the gospel that Jean was trying to spread: the genius was in the meetings. "Nothing is as good as the meetings for inspiring you to persevere," Jean said. "The Bible is in any motel room. Anybody can read the Bible, but there's a certain benefit to hearing that recited, to hear the very words you know spoken to you. Likewise, to sit in a group with people who are on the same wavelength as you is crucial."

It was the magic of the meetings that perhaps made the rigidness of the diet more tolerable. Jean thought the word *diet* suggested an easy way out; she preferred to call Weight Watchers an eating plan or a food-management program, which didn't exactly roll off the tongue. In the earliest iterations of the program, not only was there no meal skipping and no way to swap one item for another, but quantities of food were to be measured on a postal scale, and, crucially, no calories were counted. (That's the version of Weight Watchers another housewife, Betty Draper, attended on the "Dark Shadows" episode of the TV drama *Mad Men*.) One woman told Jean that she had proudly brought a scale to a friend's dinner party and weighed out six ounces of roast beef and popped open a can of mushrooms to eat while the other guests helped themselves to potato salad. This was considered a success story rather than obsessive.

In retrospect the program seems zany, almost random, in its decisions about what was "legal," which was Weight Watchers–speak for what was allowed; that language extended to people who weren't in the program. They were called "civilians" because they were not fighting in the war against fat. "In my mind, Weight Watchers members are the chosen people. Civilians, those thin people who never have to worry about fat, have never been gifted the gift we've been given, and that's to find out how strong and resourceful we really are," Jean said. This terminology was also a cunning way to denote insider and outsider and foster a sense of belonging. Which is especially important for fat people, who are often stereotyped as lonely.

Dieters could have fish, white meat from poultry, eggs (as long as they were cooked without butter or oil, and never at dinner, for some reason), cheese (but no Velveeta or cream cheese), enriched white bread, and skim milk. You could have any fruit in season except bananas, cherries, watermelon, grapes (which were considered too easy to overeat), papayas, mangoes, or dried fruit. There would be no bagels, no waffles, no spaghetti, no avocado, no fried foods of any kind, no salad dressing, no peanut butter, no yogurt, no pretzels, no rice, no ketchup, no corn, no potatoes, no smoked meat, and no alcohol. You could have beef, lamb, frankfurters, dark meat from turkey or salmon three times a week. You could have fresh beets, but not pickled ones, and green beans, but only if they were french-cut so the inner beans fell out, because those were considered fattening. Liver, as many picky members bemoaned, was mandatory.

Some rival cookbooks even seemed to be commenting on Weight Watchers' success. In *Good Housekeeping's Cookbook for Calorie Watchers,* a dieter was allowed to eat her favorite foods. "The trouble is that many diets, including the fad variety, are so monotonous that it takes a saint to stick to them. There is nothing more boring than a diet that is limited to only a few foods—one, for example, that forbids you bread for a sandwich or catchup for a hamburger." The diet also listed snacks that were available for men only, including graham crackers and glazed doughnuts.

"Creative Weight Watchers prepare the best, the most delicious, and the thinningest food in the world!!" read the final line in the Weight Watchers' program manual. Recipes tended toward the wacky, unpalatable, or depressing, by today's standards, at least: An alternative to nuts was mushrooms roasted in an oven until they dried to a crisp. Dessert was an apple with flavored low-calorie soda poured over it and baked. A Danish was made from a slice of white bread cut into four triangles, topped with a mixture of cottage cheese, water, orange juice, and sugar substitute, and broiled. A suggested liver preparation was to broil it with vinegar, salt, pepper, and paprika. The Weight Watchers "popcorn" bowl consisted of green pepper, celery, cucumber, radishes, cauliflower, mushrooms, and one or two fruits cut up into small pieces. *Et voilà*—"Nibble to your heart's content!"

The original *Weight Watchers Cook Book,* which came out in 1966 and was coauthored by Felice Lippert, who had been in charge of new recipe development, nutrition, and food research since the company was founded, came from members exchanging recipes. "Don't surround yourself with temptation by buying cookies and candies. Even a four-year-old can understand if told that mommy needs his help because she wants to become his 'beautiful mommy'...What a strikingly healthy, firm-toned, happy-looking individual has been hiding under the flabbiness. Remember, it will require your desperation, your sincerity, your cooperation, and your patience." It sold 120,000 copies its first year of publication. The message was almost authoritarian, but it was clear: You had to take on Weight Watchers as your whole life or you couldn't reap the benefits. There was no in-between.

CHAPTER TEN

SHE'D HAD ENOUGH
AFTER ONE BITE

November 2017

As many times as I have tried to diet, I have tried to quit. Dieting sounds like a binary act—you're either on or off one—but in reality, it's more like a constant low-level headache. Even when I'm not actively tallying what I consume, I am evaluating it. And I am judging myself. It's a humming background reality that I can either focus on or ignore.

About a year ago, I actively tried to find peace with myself in a paradigm outside of dieting. It began with a visit to a weight-loss camp in Vermont. It hadn't even been my idea to go—an editor had heard about their unique approach to weight loss and body acceptance and asked if I would write a story about it. I was there for five days to take notes and observe but the other women there spent $13,669 per month to be coached on how to eat intuitively. Rather than focus on numbers like a typical weight-loss program, this one was unique because it aimed to teach women how to change the way they thought about food. The days were carefully structured, with classes on meal planning, goal setting, and self-care and workouts like yoga and strength training.

One night after dinner we got rewarded with dessert—the tiniest sliver of chocolate tart. But it was meant to be an exercise. After we inspected it, we were allowed one bite and told to savor it for over a minute. And then, if we wanted more, we were to take another bite and do the same thing. Eating two dainty bites of dessert or having fruit after dinner are things I have only personally experienced by watching French movies. I ate the whole thing in two bites in less than a minute, so I had a lot of time to watch everyone around me, maybe thirty women between the ages of sixteen and sixty. There was one woman at the camp who was skinny, and she happened to be the only black woman there. She decided she'd had enough after one bite. "I've had enough," she announced to the room and covered the remaining tart with her napkin. She did this at every meal. That's a dieter trick as old as Weight Watchers, similar to Jean telling members to wash their cookies, and it made me suspect she was tricking herself into thinking she was satiated. Her act seemed like a charade. And what about happiness—I'm not sure pretending to be satisfied with a tiny scrap of tart makes anyone happy. I envied Jean's ability to simply fall in line with dieting, to buckle down to a lifetime of saying no and, seemingly, never look back. Or maybe the more accurate way to look at it was that she got a little surge every time she passed up a doughnut or stepped on the scale and was pleased with the number. I am, however, a lover of easy pleasure and quantity—I question my ability to savor anything, even thinness.

Sue Roberts, an obesity researcher at Tufts University, told me it's hard for people to eat small portions of desirable foods. In an ideal world, there would be big-government solutions attuned to that. For example, restaurants would be required to sell different portion sizes with proportionate prices. So if a slice of the original cheesecake at the Cheese-cake Factory was 830 calories, they would have to offer a smaller one that was, say, 400 calories for about half the price, and a no doubt tiny one for 200 calories for about a quarter of the original price. Roberts assured me this future ideal is unlikely ever to happen in the United States; without fail I would eat the whole thing because desserts are delicious. But if given the option, I probably would buy a smaller slice. Not every time, but sometimes. When Roberts supervises dieters herself, she aims for a much higher satiety diet of foods that taste similar to what you like so it's filling, yet has some eating structure. For example, if you have a sweet tooth, you can have chocolate but you have to melt a square of dark chocolate on high-fiber cereal so it's the taste you crave mixed with fiber to slow digestion. Or you can have a square (one square!) of dark chocolate after dinner, but you have to chase it with mint tea—chocolate cannot be the snack in and of itself; it can't be your first or last taste, and you can never eat it alone. You're supposed to savor the flavor and take small bites so that the one little square you're eating tastes like more than it is.

For the amount of money that (thankfully) was not coming out of my own pocket, I had expected that camp to be lavish, like a spa in Arizona where they have cold towels waiting for you after a morning hike. On a lush and secluded patch of property in the mountains, the place felt like what I imagine rehab might be like. When I arrived, I entered through a small main room where a group of women was gathered watching *The Bachelor*. They all swiveled their heads to check me out, the new inmate in fat-person prison. My room was dark and looked like it belonged in a dilapidated highway motel. I felt a pang in my chest I hadn't for decades—homesickness. I wanted to get out of there and went so far as to look up train times for the next morning. The austerity of the place reminded me of the fat camp I went to as a kid. I spent a long time flossing my teeth and rubbing in moisturizer and talking myself down; it was just a few days and I had a story to report. At the very least, I figured, I would lose weight. Maybe going to a spa was too much like vacationing, anyway. Maybe what I needed was some tough love and a dumpy room.

I was ostensibly at the camp to take a class on body neutrality, which is the idea that you can reach a kind of détente, a white flag, a way station between hating and loving yourself. Late in the afternoon after I arrived, I sat with a group of women, who ranged from college age to their forties, in a meeting led by the program director, whose previous job was running the fitness program at an elite East Coast college. She had prompted everyone to consider "what your body felt like and looked like at different times in your life." Everyone was jotting notes down in a binder with the program's "womanifesto" printed on it ("Too often, our lives play out on the stage between our ears"). A blonde in her thirties talked about being a former competitive swimmer who felt shame because she gained weight; a brunette next to her talked about how, despite losing half her body weight in college, she always felt obese.

Our teacher listened to all of this and nodded. "There's a whole movement talking about loving our bodies. But it's kind of a long jump to move there from dissatisfaction," she said. "Some people are just going to land in body neutrality, which is the term we utilize here for somewhere in the middle." The way I will feel about my body, like my weight, will always fluctuate. And wanting to be fit isn't antithetical to body neutrality, nor is dieting. Body neutrality isn't a license to throw in the towel, dive headfirst into a pile of chips, and give up on feeling healthy; it's a way to move on from the mind-set of needing to lose weight or worrying about what you see in the mirror to focusing on how you feel. It's chasing what feels good, what you think you need in the moment.

After teaching, the program director sat down with me and talked about her personal history. "My journey is yo-yo dieting, diet after diet, and never happy with my body. I'm tired and I don't like how much it has occupied my whole life." She called all the space that food talk takes up in her brain "Judge Foodie." When asked about whether she had gotten to body acceptance, she shook her head no. "I honor and respect my body. I like feeling strong, certain things I like, but I can't say I love it." That didn't sound like a failure; the revelation that she was making her way through the spectrum of body hate to body love and currently fell somewhere in the middle made it sound more real and more achievable. "Body neutrality is experiential and not something that happens overnight," she told me. "It's one awareness at a time, one thought at a time."

The thing is, I'm not sure anybody is or can be neutral about their bodies. The minute you observe anything, it's not neutral. In fact, going to a camp is pretty extreme. There was something of Marie Antoinette playacting shepherdess at the Petit Trianon about the whole thing, these rich women who could afford to spend the money and take the time away from their lives for a month (sometimes more than that, and some people were repeat customers) to do nothing but concentrate on their bodies. It's unrealistic for most people, who would probably prefer to pay off loans, boost their quality of life, pay off their credit cards, or save that money. Even if it could be spent freely, they could go on vacation or buy a cashmere wardrobe or a car or, in some places, a house.

I got home from the camp on a Friday afternoon, starving. I didn't have any groceries and sat with a food-delivery app open, paralyzed over what to order. What did I want? What did my body want? Those questions were too loaded to answer on an empty stomach. I ended up ordering a salad and some french fries. It's one of my favorite comfort-food combinations. I never know if I should feel virtuous or like a failure eating it. Maybe I'll never find moral salvation in my food.

How good does it sound to just not care, to eat what I like and not feel bad about it? The same summer I went to the weight-loss camp in Vermont—before my Weight Watchers year—I traveled to the Body Love Conference in Arizona. Just going felt a little bit defeatist, like body love was an attempt to cut my losses, to tell myself I was not willing to feel like a failure by dieting any longer and that I would try to find a way to appreciate myself as I was. Even though admission was just twenty-five dollars and the conference was held at a community college, there was a kind of bountifulness to it. (It's fascinating that it didn't cost a lot to be abundant at the Body Love Conference but austerity in Vermont was expensive.) CHANGE YOUR WORLD. LOVE YOUR BODY! read the movie theater–size screen looming over a standing-room-only crowd of around three hundred people, mostly women: suburban-mom types, pierced-septum alt-college students, and what appeared to be a handful of walk-of-shamers decked out in sparkles and miniskirts at nine a.m. It was approaching 100 degrees outside, so no one was wearing much. There were a lot of sundresses, and there was a lot of skin. Most of the people attending were fat or at least chubby; I imagined that many of the other attendees wouldn't mind being called that.

During a vegan-Mexican catered lunch, one conference attendee who had come all the way from Yellowknife, in subarctic Canada, told me she'd found acceptance by challenging herself to wear a bikini for thirty days everywhere she went in her town: "First I wore it in bed, then to dinner, then in the yard," she said. "A guy in a bar told me"—while she was wearing a bikini at said bar—"'I really believe in what you're doing and it's important.' I walk around saying, 'I am beautiful and everyone loves me,' and have noticed that the world has responded to me completely differently." I appreciated her chutzpah but even that stunt wasn't going to solve my problems.

At a session entitled "Silent No More: Speaking the Body's Stories," a performance artist wearing a nude bodysuit wrote *fat* on her belly, *queer* on her arm, *lazy* and *disabled* on her legs, and *freak* on her chest while doing a ballet-ish dance. She read a poem with the lines "We are the women who eat pain like tattoos" and "Our tears turn to crystals." Then audience members were invited to come to the stage and cut her out of her suit while Nina Simone played in the background. I left early to get a free chair massage from a local massage school. That was probably the highlight of my day.

The hardest kind of mind-twisting thinking came at a breakout session called "No More 'Weighting,'" where a dietitian and a therapist advised the audience to "focus on health and self-care, and let your body sort it out." The first person who raised her hand to make a comment cried. She used the words *trauma issues* and *trigger* when talking about the gym. It reminded me of some of the less successful women's studies courses I took in college that devolved into group therapy. A girl seated behind me said, "I want a plan for not making a plan." That brought up the question I was intending to ask: If you give up dieting and all its attendant actions, what do you do next? How do you make it through the period that comes between quitting dieting and, well, loving yourself? The response was a deeply unsatisfying non-answer: "That's the work," said the nutritionist. "Say, 'I'm taking a pause from this dieting paradigm; I'm going to focus more on healing than changing.' Focus on radical self-care." Essentially, their answer was the same as the bikini woman's: Fake it till you make it. Pretend you're comfortable in your body until you are. Give yourself time to get there.

That same year I had enrolled myself in a sixteen-week on-line program called Stop Fighting Food started by a former dieter turned nutrition coach, who proclaimed, "I help women stop feeling crazy about food...No yo-yo dieting, no drastic swings; just me, having a life, and not letting food ruin it." The program agreement specified that the woman who ran it was not a doctor, dietitian, therapist, nutritionist, or psychologist—that she was not, in fact, any kind of licensed professional at all. I read this, and then allowed my mother to hand over $1,275—because when I called the program director to discuss signing up, she had said, "I think my program can help you." That's all it took for me to tune out my analytical mind and any natural skepticism in hopes of finding some peace with my body.

Phase one of the class involved a few online lectures a week; three conference calls in which our leader, my twenty-some classmates, and I could discuss roadblocks; and a Facebook group I was encouraged to join about Intuitive Eating— more or less the idea that when you remove "good" or "bad" stigmas around specific foods and give yourself permission to eat anything you want, cravings and bingeing fade away. This approach was made popular by a 1995 book called *Intuitive Eating: A Revolutionary Program That Works* written by a dietitian and a nutrition coach. After three months of trying that, I learned that I'll never *not* want to eat Chubby Hubby, that I will unfailingly choose fried chicken or enchiladas over salad, and that, given a green light to eat what I want when I want it, I will gain fifteen pounds and won't feel any better about myself.

The second phase of the class revolved around body

positivity. I was asked to give my body a name and to treat "her" well. I tried for ten minutes to think of a name I could deal with. Iris? (A name I have always thought would be good for a daughter.) Jane? (Normal, like the body I wanted.) Chantilly? (My favorite name as a child that I later learned is French for "whipped cream.") I couldn't do it; feeling less than unqualified joy about what I see in the mirror is unavoidable. "If you're even a tiny bit of a critical person, there are always things that are wrong with everything. We have this notion of love that is connected to perfectionism—the image that we should be in bliss all the time is so strong in our culture," Joan Chrisler, a professor of psychology at Connecticut College in New London, told me. "What might instead be a more successful and realistic approach is to think, You have the body you have, and accept what you have. It's an essential part of yourself."

Harriet Brown, who has written a great deal about weight and eating disorders, was another voice of reason. She said when I phoned her that it was okay to admit that all of this felt ridiculous. "For me, standing in front of the mirror and saying, 'I love my butt'—there's part of me that says, 'No, I don't.' So it's pointless," Brown said. And when I put my question to her—how was I supposed to love my body?—she was equally blunt. "That's the wrong answer to the wrong question, really. You can't just decide to love anything. The process before you can get to that is to let go of self-loathing. You might end up loving your body, or not." The forward motion, she said, "is doing activities that are going to make you healthier that don't have anything to do with losing weight."

At least it was something to work toward. Positive affirmations were not new to me, but even when I made a halfhearted attempt to look in the mirror and praise, say, my Cupid's bow lips, I kept thinking that people who were truly beautiful didn't need to do remedial exercises. My greatest disappointment was that, if the class Facebook page was any indication—although people have certainly been known to lie on social media—my classmates seemed to be undergoing a paradigm shift en masse. I could practically hear the synapses in their brains firing. One woman reported she was shopping for a bikini to wear on vacation for the first time; another triumphantly got rid of jeans that were too small. I felt more frustrated than when I'd begun.

Surely all of this is complicated by my personal politics. For as long as I can remember, I've considered myself a feminist. When I am actively dieting, the guilt I once felt about what I ate becomes replaced by guilt over being the wrong kind of feminist—or maybe no kind of feminist, a woman pursuing something as conventional and ennui-inducing as losing weight. I fear that instead of fighting for a world where all bodies are admired, I'm pandering, reshaping my body to make it acceptable to the world around me. There's a thread of old-school feminist thought that says taking pleasure in being admired for our looks is participating in our own oppression, minimizing our brains and power. One of the most nuanced takes on food and society and feminism I've read is in Judith Warner's book *Perfect Madness:* "It was as though there were good and bad kinds of controlling behavior. The bad kind was the kind that played into the hands of the 'patriarchy'—promoting thinness, for example, or anything else that conformed to what was generally considered male notions of female beauty. The good kind took on the patriarchy—in the form of challenging the medical establishment, the food industry, or anything else that smacked of convention." All these behaviors, she argues, make us feel good; there is a self-reinforcing aspect to it. "Food-and-body control is an opiate. A highly effective and highly adaptive way of drowning out the angst of existence."

Liberated women are fully aware of the complicated politics involved in food, fat, and our bodies. We know how corrupt the diet industry is; we take to social media to applaud brands for expanding their plus-size lines. Most of us agree that the insurance charts for what is considered a healthy weight are unrealistic, that the standard definition of beauty is criminally narrow. We have a surplus of knowledge, and perhaps because of this, the only publicly acceptable message is one of body positivity and self-acceptance.

Good feminists, in short, do not diet. Or if they do, they don't talk about it. We are trained to hide our dieting, or to make our dieting look less like dieting, because we are supposed to know better. A writer I know lived in fear that a guy she was dating would spot the prepackaged low-calorie food from a diet delivery service in her freezer; another tries to count her cashews away from her coworkers. Another friend has a private, secret Instagram just so she can follow fitness accounts.

I believe in body love. I also believe, beyond the personal ramifications of self-love and body positivity as a political act, that we all deserve space. I believe that for some women, being kind to themselves works. I do. But for me, the body-acceptance rhetoric just doesn't hold up to any level of intellectual rigor. If I have not been able to rely on my body to do what I wanted it to and to please me, I have been able to rely on my brain. So an exercise meant to make me feel better in my body, such as positive affirmations, has to appeal to my intellect before it gets to my emotions.

Our bodies are more complicated than body positivity. The radical body-love movement is an essential counterpoint to the prevailing, persistent aesthetic of super-fit and slim, but it's also unrealistic; it takes a rare pioneer to truly flout beauty norms. And I am no dissenter. I'm not sure it's the answer for me if it means it is not okay to want to be *not fat*. My desire never wavers. Maybe my biggest problems are with the very words *love* and *positivity* and *neutrality* and *acceptance* themselves. As if trying to manage my body isn't difficult enough, it presumes I am going to have a handle on how I feel. Loving my body still keeps the focus on my body. What I would prefer to have is the freedom not to think about my body at all.

The most magical way of thinking is one I can't seem to give up: That it's going to be different this time. Dieting is asking you to control something wild and ungovernable, your body, with your brain, which is only slightly more under your control. Diet companies, including Weight Watchers, know we are repeat customers. The average weight loss in behavior-modification programs is only about 5 percent over six months, and most participants will gain one-third of that weight back after two years. It's nearly impossible to lose a significant amount of weight and keep it off, so impossible that people who do manage to do it are studied by scientists. I'm aware that the house always wins! And in this case the house is both diet companies and my fat body. I'm as cynical as they come, but I also think, over and over, this could be the one time the diet sticks, that the numbers on the scale go down and stay there, that I'm cured. I still think that I'm not thin because I don't want it bad enough, that I'm not dedicated enough, that I'm simply not trying hard enough. But is that true? I have certainly worked my way to the top of a really competitive industry. And yet I probably think of nothing as often as I think of food and dieting.

I keep going back to dieting not just to achieve weight loss but because it's all I know. For someone raised without religion, dieting has been a source of faith. At least, it is the structure of my life. Without dieting, my life would lack organization. I can rely on the familiar path of dieting for dealing with problems that are huge, like my body and confidence. It's the way station through which I earn love, both from myself and from the outside world. If I were to surrender to a life without dieting, it would be like losing faith in myself. I don't know if I can feel confident despite the shape of my body or learn to love my body despite my lack of confidence in it. My assessment of my body has always been linked to my confidence. I realize the two are separate, but I have never experienced them unlinked.

Jean didn't even like the word *diet!* Because a diet isn't something you pursue for a few months until you reach your goal; it's not a short-term solution that you can buckle down for to solve a long-term problem like weight. A term like *lifestyle change* is a more accurate description of the process.

But it's just another euphemism. A more fitting word for the state of mind that weight loss and its maintenance require is *vigilance,* which you must practice constantly.

But as much as dieting frustrates me and as much as I see, clear-eyed, how impossible it is, I still pursue it because at least I know what diet success looks like.

And my commitment to Weight Watchers was paying off, slowly. I'd lost eight pounds, which was fine, but it seemed slow because my clothes still didn't feel different and the world wasn't treating me differently. Being in the middle of a transformation doesn't necessarily feel good. At the age of forty, I was slowly coming to suspect that my life wasn't going to take a sharp turn into a fairy tale. But I'd have been happy with one makeover scene. You don't get everything you want, and sometimes your longed-for transformation shows the cracks in your plans, shining a light on the new problems that sprout in place of old ones. What you thought you wanted isn't what you end up with. You have to accept what's on the menu and order from there.

I had my first biweekly personal coaching session, a feature of my subscription plan—a Weight Watchers coach called you and for fifteen minutes, you could troubleshoot your week in as much agonizing detail as you wished and get some practical feedback. "I am embarrassed about how hard I'm trying and how I'm doing just mediocre. I would give myself a C plus, maybe a B minus," I told Miriam. Her advice was to be less hung up on the mental aspect of losing weight, the "why" in particular. Miriam was a leader who was very attuned to how people felt—I imagined her emotional intelligence was off the charts—but, like Jean, she was professionally interested in practical solutions. She was fond of saying things like "Not all meals have to be celebrations. Just because you woke up in the morning doesn't mean you get rewarded with croissants. And if you do eat a croissant, lunch will be a salad with all zero-point ingredients."

Weight Watchers, even done one-on-one, was not therapy. Getting out of my head seemed like a good idea. "*Why* is a very judgmental word, even one referring to yourself," Miriam said. Her advice was the opposite of mind-twisting exercises in loving yourself and was, instead, entirely prescriptive: Be okay with drinking more caffeine if that was how I was coping that week; look at the Weight Watchers website and the app for recipe ideas; guess how greasy a meal eaten at a restaurant was by how much residual oil was on the plate and record my points accordingly. I got off the phone elated, the same way I felt when I left therapy. I wanted to please her possibly more than I wanted to please myself. Or maybe Miriam was just added motivation. Regardless, I could feel myself falling for her, wanting to make her my guru, my own present-day Jean.

The next night I went to a dinner at the Polo Lounge, the restaurant on the Upper East Side owned by Ralph Lauren, which was celebrating some kind of annual steak harvest from Mr. Lauren's ranch in Colorado. I ate plenty but didn't gorge myself, not on steak, not on wine, not even on pecan pie. It was like I was pretending to be a normal person.

Three days later I was back at Weight Watchers listening to Miriam say, "My grandfather always said, gamblers do not lose bungalow colonies." I think the message was that only gambling addicts do that and that we should assess what we do for comfort and what our coping mechanisms are. Patrice the judge said that she was "a need-to-know person. I do not mess around." I believe she was talking about the points in a turkey sandwich. She was celebrating finally reaching a healthy BMI range with one of these dumb sparkly stickers they give you like you're in elementary school. "I can't believe I lost," she said, shaking her head. "I was at a bar association dinner. I don't remember how many lamb chops and duck wraps I had after I drank a glass of sangria. But that was it—I don't want lawyers to see me drinking, considering what I do for a living." She was still twelve pounds over her goal weight. This was her third time at Weight Watchers. I asked her how this attempt was going. "Menopause is a bitch," she said. "Just you wait."

I was scared to weigh myself—I always am; I can't imagine stepping on a scale and not having it fill me with dread—but I was down 2.4 more pounds, for a total of just over 10 pounds. All that, and I had English muffins with melted cheese every day for breakfast. Rosemarie said that her mother joined Weight Watchers but with the stipulation she would not stop eating the cinnamon roll she bought at the Italian bakery on the way to work every morning. And she made it work; she planned her food for the day around it.

I raised my hand and told the room a story of my own. A few nights before, I had been ten minutes into an at-home spin class and heard something loud hitting my building. It turned out to be paint balls. I got up to clean them and ended up locked out of my building wearing nothing but a sports bra and leggings and socks in 30-degree weather. Twenty minutes later one of my neighbors came home and let me in, after which I changed my outfit and went right back to the class. Everyone clapped for me and I felt a pang of real joy.

Was I making it work? Was this a lifestyle? All of us probably had a lot to learn from one another, as trite and sentimental as that sounded. Miriam followed up by telling us that when her mother was very young, she attended a one-room schoolhouse. "And this space is like a one-room schoolhouse too," she said, "where everyone is together but we're all at different levels."

CHAPTER ELEVEN

THIN POWER

1969

Heavies beware! No one is safe once Jean socks it to them," declared an article in *Look* magazine from May 27, 1969. Jean Nidetch's star was on the rise and the biweekly publication, which was known for its pictures, decided to capture her in her prime. There were plenty of photos of Jean: mobbed in crowds, wearing a dress by Emilio Pucci with her arms spread wide in almost messianic pose, playing golf, at home with Marty, posing in front of old photos of herself when she was fat. The writer Louis Botto and photographer Phillip Harrington followed her to Louisville ("in the high protein province, Jean spreads her gospel"), where they encountered quite a scene. "Mrs. Nidetch was surrounded by fans at the airport, while former Vice President Humphrey, who is an honorary Weight Watcher, scarcely attracted notice. Obviously, she carries more weight." Fans were everywhere. The *Look* story described a night out with her and Marty dancing at the wedding of a "shrunken" bride. Jean now had the money and was small enough to wear anything she wanted, and she leaned toward the flamboyant: flared trapeze coats, midi-skirts, big black glasses, marabou-trimmed sleeves, turbans. She showed up to a meeting and was greeted by zealous fans carrying signs that read KEEP THE FAITH, JEAN BABY; BE LEAN WITH JEAN; FATTERY WILL GET YOU NOWHERE; HIPS HIPS AWAY; IF YOU INDULGE YOU'RE GONNA BULGE; BODY BY WEIGHT WATCHERS; TAKE IT OFF, TAKE IT OFF, TAKE IT ALL OFF; THINK THIN, EAT THIN, BE THIN; IT'S ONLY A MATTER OF MIND OVER BATTER; GIRLS DON'T MAKE EYES AT FAT GUYS; and DON'T SUBSCRIBE TO THE FEEDER'S DIGEST.

First Jean was thin, then she was famous, and now she was rich. She made enough money to buy her entire Queens apartment building—she wanted to stay in the area for her sons, who were still in school—and kept maids on staff. She had it all, and she was basking in it. "For a while, you know, I got egotistical about it. Oh, I'm Marilyn Monroe, I thought. I am a star. I remember being filled with ego," she said. "And then one day I was getting off a plane, surrounded by crowds of people, and my handbag strap broke. I watched my compact fall, then my mirror, my wallet. And I thought—God just told me who I am. I am not Marilyn Monroe. I am a lady who got thin and now I have to tell the world about it."

She had recently been made a consultant to the New York State Assembly Mental Hygiene Committee, and she liked to add *FFH,* for "formerly fat housewife," to her name—something she adopted following a medical conference where she was the only one without a title or initials after her name. She was Weight Watchers' mascot, spokeswoman, and evangelist. "I am," she said, "essentially a salesman." She was traveling all over the country visiting Weight Watchers franchises and meeting leaders, all of whom had to have lost weight so they could remember what it was like to be fat and how difficult it was to lose weight. There were even babies named after her. And she met people on the program, so many that, inspired by McDonald's tally of how many customers it served, Weight Watchers had a 1969 campaign with the slogan "More than 17 million pounds lost." Bringing "before" pictures to meetings was strongly encouraged. There were at least two Weight Watchers weddings as of 1967 and plenty of charming success stories to be shared with the press: the nineteen-year-old boy who was 323 pounds when he joined and lost 200; the guy who wandered into a meeting at the Paramount Hotel in New York and stayed because he met a pretty girl there and kept coming because he wanted to see her again. She graduated from the program and left but he still ended up losing 65 pounds.

By March 1964, less than a year after the first meeting, Weight Watchers had thirty-three classes across the New York metro area. They began franchising beyond New York City almost immediately. Al Lippert's idea was to sell the franchises for a low amount, sometimes just $2,000, but franchise holders—all of whom were Weight Watchers graduates and many of whom were women with an investment in the company that was not just fiscal but emotional—were contractually obligated to pay Weight Watchers 10 percent of their gross, which sometimes came to as much as $100,000 per year. "It's like giving away razors to sell razor blades," Lippert said. By 1969, Jean and the Lipperts had 102 franchises in the United States, Canada, Puerto Rico, Great Britain, and Israel, totaling about 1.5 million members. In September 1968, Weight Watchers went public and reported a gross revenue of $5.5 million. In its initial public offering of 225,000 shares, its stock rose from an initial price of $11.25 a share to $30.00 on its first day of trading. Jean didn't think of herself as a money person or someone who had a head for business.

When Florine Mark visited New York City to attend Weight Watchers, she met the Lipperts, who suggested she start a location in Detroit. It seemed like a good idea. After all, the program was working for her, plus she was looking for some direction and needed money to put her kids through college. She started her franchise with one meeting on a Tuesday and thirty people came—her family and a few older people. She made a sign advertising the meetings and went to a candy store—where else to find people who might be struggling with food? she reasoned—and convinced the guy working there to let her put it up. The next week a few more people came, then there were sixty the next week, and then two hundred the next month. Soon Florine Mark's WW Group became the largest Weight Watchers franchise with locations in fourteen states and three countries.

Weight Watchers became so ubiquitous that Jessica Mitford thought the time was right to investigate the company. Mitford was an aristocratic British journalist and the second youngest of the six Mitford sisters (there were seven siblings: Nancy, Pamela, Diana, Unity, Jessica, Deborah, and a brother named Thomas, all born between 1904 and 1920). Their adult lives were a mirror of the political, psychosocial hegemony of the twentieth century; the journalist Ben Macintyre helpfully summed them up as "Diana the Fascist, Jessica the Communist, Unity the Hitler-lover; Nancy the Novelist; Deborah the Duchess and Pamela the unobtrusive poultry connoisseur." Jessica was the only one to live in the United States, in the San Francisco Bay Area with her civil rights lawyer husband, Robert Treuhaft. She had published a scathing exposé of the funeral industry, *The American Way of Death*, in 1963.

In her 1967 article on Weight Watchers for the *New York Post* (which was syndicated around the country), Jessica Mitford began with skepticism about diet companies. "The before-and-after photo is one of the most familiar advertising clichés. A monstrous mound of a woman, generally overflowing in a bathing suit, and presto! There she is, a glamorous size 12 in sequined gown." She mentioned gullible women, pills, expensive mechanical-slimming contraptions, and exercise salons preying on the desperate and naive. Mitford saw a "before" and "after" of Jean that a friend had jokingly put on her refrigerator as a warning and inspiration for her overweight teen daughters. Mitford was suspicious of the photo, the chunky and frumpy brunette turned into a willowy blonde. "How does Weight Watchers work?" Mitford asked. Her friend said it was similar to Alcoholics Anonymous. "I suppose if you yearn for an eclair in the middle of the night, you call up your buddy and she talks you into a stalk of celery instead," she figured. "Is Weight Watchers just another device to separate the fool from his (or more likely her) money?"

Mitford used the expansion of Weight Watchers into San Francisco as the peg for her story. She visited that city's first meeting, attended by eight hundred "too solid citizens." It was held on a warm summer evening near Golden Gate Park, a place, she pointed out, in hilarious period detail, that "is normally populated by groups of beaded and sandaled hippies, wandering through the trees hand in hand and sitting about the lawns with their guitars." Mitford, who was thin herself, didn't have a great deal of sympathy for the fat. "The hugely obese, while they exclude themselves from most forms of public recreation, are drawn together by their common passion for eating." Weight Watchers catered to the fat, not women looking to shave off a few pounds to resemble the popular rail-thin fashion model Twiggy. Her verdict: "I came to scoff, but I stayed to applaud."

Later she met Jean, who was staying at the storied Fairmont Hotel. Jean liked the attention and told Mitford, "I love all the glamour and publicity, it's the most ego-inflating thing in the world." That day Jean was wearing a formfitting Italian knit suit and looked like "the original bombshell mixed with a dash of Phyllis Diller," Mitford wrote. "She speaks with the sure touch and gift of timing of a gifted comic or a seasoned vaudeville star." Jean's suite was decorated for the duration of her stay with her own portraits, some life-size, and she was busy the whole time taking calls from television and radio producers and reporters who wanted to interview her. "There is something very disarming about the way Jean Nidetch revels, with frank and unabashed delight, in her new-found fame and fortune."

Jean, for her part, claimed not to know who Mitford was— not as a journalist or activist or a member of a famous family. She had done the reporting under her married name, Jessica

Treuhaft. Even if Jean didn't know who she was, surely someone at Weight Watchers knew who Jessica Mitford was. Either way, Jean was proud, and maybe even a little relieved, at the resulting story. "She had originally come to expose us, and she found there was nothing to expose."

It was all part of a phenomenon that psychiatrist Albert J. Stunkard would call in 1973 "a national neurosis" that "has grown from a mild concern to an overriding preoccupation"; the 1960s saw a kind of Weight Watchers explosion. By 1967 the *New York Times* reported that there were 297 classes per week in New York City alone. (The success of her company did not prevent Jean from being identified in the article as "Mrs. Marty Nidetch.") There was a Weight Watchers restaurant on Forty-Ninth Street between Madison Avenue and Fifth Avenue where you could order a Bloody Shame (a virgin Bloody Mary). Lippert came up with a kind of portable folder with packets of artificial sweetener, bouillon, and powdered skim milk that they branded themselves for weight watching on the go. There was a frozen-food line with a picture of thin Jean right on the box. Indianapolis mayor Richard Lugar proclaimed a "Jean Nidetch Day." There was a life insurance plan endorsed by Weight Watchers with premiums that went down as you lost weight.

Weight Watchers began to target men with male-only sessions, the idea being that men would more easily open up about their issues with food and their bodies "when there were no female discussions involving dress sizes, etc., to distract them," Jean wrote. A Weight Watchers ad from 1969 showed a photograph of a middle-aged man in a suit stuck in a swivel chair with a caption that read, "An executive should carry extra weight on his shoulders. But not on his hips." The 1973 printing of the *Weight Watchers Program Cookbook* included an augmented meal plan for men that allowed for two extra servings of fruit per day, an extra slice of bread at breakfast and lunch, and an additional two ounces of fish, meat, or poultry at dinner.

In February of 1968 the first issue of *Weight Watchers* magazine, published by the same people who brought us the *National Lampoon,* hit the stands with 300,000 copies. Inside was a mix of lighthearted fare, fashion and beauty stories, and reported pieces revolving around weight loss. "Meet My Mother...the Girl" was the story of a woman who lost 150 pounds and "gained a new life." "How to Slim Your Face with Makeup" was basically a lesson on how to contour, and "Vacation Bound" was a fashion spread, although the clothes didn't look remotely like they were plus-size, and neither did the models. The message was to dress to hide unwanted pounds; "a flattering coat with a vertical band" would make you look taller and slimmer. And there was a lot of food: a primer on herbs and spices, recipes for poached sole rolls, sweetbread casserole, and veal tenderloin, and a lot of "legal" Weight Watchers desserts. "One of the nicest things about these fabulous desserts is that those of us who are watching our weight can enjoy them, too. With so many tasty foods available, there's no reason to do without the treat that makes a happy ending to a good meal," read the copy introducing recipes and photos of croquembouche melon, pear Jacqueline, peach melba, and granita de café.

Food was also the source of the magazine's first and biggest scandal. In its second issue, in March 1968, it ran an article titled "Jackie Kennedy's Gourmet Chef Presents Her Weight Watchers Recipes." In it, Annemarie Huste, the private chef to the always thin former First Lady, shared recipes for lemon broiled chicken, Spanish melon, raspberries à l'orange, baked tomatoes, and a Bibb salad with just lettuce, parsley, chives, tarragon, and some fresh lemon juice squeezed on top.

An editor at *Weight Watchers* magazine had met the young, attractive German chef Annemarie Huste on a ski weekend and suggested the magazine would like to publish some of her Continental-inspired recipes for cold lobster or maybe quiche Lorraine. Huste agreed, with the stipulation that no mention would be made of her employer Jacqueline—Huste had signed an agreement when she had been hired two years before, saying she wouldn't write about the family. Mattie Simmons, the magazine's editor, said she didn't know Huste had such an agreement but also that "Mrs. Kennedy wasn't even mentioned in the article," which was technically true, since her name was only in the title and on the cover. Kennedy was furious—she felt like it was a Jackie diet that she hadn't endorsed and didn't want to. She summoned her lawyers to try to get the piece stopped but they had learned of it when the issue was already in print.

Huste retained powerful legal counsel of her own, Roy M. Cohn, the famous lawyer who had represented Senator Joseph McCarthy. "I was so humiliated and furious. I called my lawyer and he told me to just apologize to Mrs. Kennedy," she told a reporter. Kennedy's response was "You should have known better." But she dropped it and didn't actually fire her. At least until a week or so later. Huste passed a newsstand and saw a copy of the *New York Post* proclaiming her cooking was responsible for Kennedy dropping two dress sizes. "It was all made up and I was scared to death," she said to the press, denying her participation in the tabloid story. She called Nancy Tuckerman, Kennedy's secretary, who told Huste, "Under the circumstances Mrs. Kennedy felt you had better not come back to work."

Huste hadn't been protective enough of the Kennedy mystique and was perhaps too ambitious. Kennedy had once chided her for being too impressed by money and power. "Isn't everybody?" was Huste's response. Publishers came calling for a tell-all, which Huste refused to give, comparing her job to being a doctor or a lawyer in terms of discretion. But she did want to write a recipe book. *Annemarie's Personal Cookbook* came out in the fall of 1968 with detailed instructions on how to make loin lamb chops seasoned with salt, pepper, and a squeeze of lemon and how she'd worked for a certain little boy—strongly hinting at John F. Kennedy Jr.— who loved artichokes.

The Kennedy diet scandal was probably the apex of star power for *Weight Watchers* magazine. From time to time there was an interview with someone whose name is still recognizable today, but the interviews always revolved uncharitably around weight, to the exclusion of other subjects. The songwriter Burt Bacharach "Tells Me How to Dress Thin"; an interview with hairstylist Vidal Sassoon: "'I work with the bones of the face,' he said, leaning back in a leather lounge chair still warm from a recent customer's leg waxing. 'If a woman came to me with her bone structure covered by several layers of fat, I would tell her to go home, lose

40 pounds and *then* come back.'" A fashion story with the young stars playing Tevye's daughters from the Broadway production of *Fiddler on the Roof* featured a very young Bette Midler modeling mod outfits of the era: an apple-green shirtdress, red patent-leather shoes, and knee socks.

The recipes for Weight Watchers–approved food were either ascetic or oddly unpalatable. A spread in *Weight Watchers* magazine featured a buffet luncheon at the New York club El Morocco, where they served Chicken Jean, a mere chicken breast baked with some mushrooms and dill, and Thin 'N Tonics, just six ounces of low-calorie tonic water with a slice of lime. A proposed Thanksgiving menu consisted of clam broth, roast turkey breast, cauliflower with pimento sauce, mashed parsnips, rhubarb relish, and chilled squash for dessert. Tropical Treasure was frozen green beans blended with orange juice, lemon juice, coconut extract, banana extract, nonfat dry milk powder, artificial sweetener, and mint, then baked at 350 degrees for thirty minutes. There was mackerel-cantaloupe salad with pickles and "frankfurter spectacular" with sliced hot dogs on top of fruit salad. Imitation foods were in nearly every issue. Mock-coconut macaroons were made with frozen cauliflower, instant coffee, coconut extract, artificial sweetener, and salt. Drawn "butter" was unflavored gelatin, water, imitation butter flavoring, nonfat dry milk, salt, and yellow food coloring. "Avocado" dip was made of canned asparagus, celery, dehydrated onion, salt, pepper, Tabasco sauce, and lemon juice. A prizewinning reader recipe from February 1970 was "french fries" made of canned green beans cooked until crunchy. As cheerful as the magazine wanted to make dieting seem, the recipes would invariably be a rejection of most people's favorite foods and, thus, a rejection of their former selves.

In Jean's monthly advice column, she responded to reader queries in her chatty way that was suffused with a great deal of tough love. The questions usually broke down into several recurring themes. One was frustration with the weight or eating habits of family and friends. A mother in Palm Beach wrote, "I have a baby less than 2 years old. He weighed 11 pounds at birth and is very very heavy now—even though he is adorable. Do you feel that he is too young for Weight Watching?" Jean encouraged the letter writer to teach him that a cookie does not equal happiness because "obesity is never cute, and even in the case of a baby it can never be considered pretty, attractive, or healthy." Another frequent query was from people writing in from a city or country where there were no Weight Watchers meetings, wondering how to still follow the diet. To a reader who complained that the nearest center was sixty miles away, Jean responded that if she really wanted to lose weight badly enough "60 miles should be a walk around the block." Many letters asked if certain foods were legal on the plan or if substitutions could be made. The answer was always no. "I never agree to substitutions of any kind, simply because if you start by substituting a roll for two slices of bread, you will invariably substitute a sliver of cake for the roll and then a chunk of cake for the sliver," Jean wrote. In another column she noted that "French pastry is an allergic food for me—I break out in fat."

Through the magazine's pages, you can see how Weight Watchers responded to changing times. In 1972 it published

"A Concise Guide to Women's Lib" by Lucianne Goldberg and also featured a big ad for *Ms.* magazine. *Ms.*'s cofounder Gloria Steinem was photographed with Jean in a photo that ran alongside the June 1972 Ask Jean Nidetch column. There was a fashion spread for working mothers. "Do you work? Are you starting a career or returning to a job after raising a family? Office clothes, which once might have posed a problem to the woman who doesn't want to or can't afford to or has no room to maintain two wardrobes, have caught up with the times," the copy read. "The working woman can't be put into a mold. She might be an executive secretary, or a gal Friday, or a file clerk, or teacher, or stockbroker, or the trusted right hand of an important executive or she might be the boss herself."

The counterculture of the late 1960s made an occasional, often humorous appearance as well. In "A Primer for the Single Girl" in 1968, there were anthropological sketches of the types of guys single girls would encounter over the summer, including "the weekend hippie," who turns out to be a kind of sleaze in bellbottoms. "His favorite expressions are 'scene,' 'bag' and 'transcendental meditation' which he may offer to explain to you if you will accompany him to a spiritually secluded spot." An anonymous writer turned to Jean with a unique query about whether one could smoke marijuana on Weight Watchers. "See, I'm considered a hippie, a real freak with the hair and bells and the whole bit...So, I've got a question—is dope okay on your program. Let's see how cool the founder of Weight Watchers is. Well, thanks, and peace." Jean, it turns out, wasn't all that groovy. "Your letter involves a very serious and widespread problem...Of course the smoking of marijuana has no relation whatsoever to the Weight Watchers program...I guess I'm not the kind of cool person you want me to be. But it's my choice...and I feel very cool, indeed, having lost 72 pounds." A reader wrote in to *Weight Watchers* magazine wondering if there was a way for the svelte to celebrate themselves. No doubt inspired by the idea of Black Power, the reader suggested Thin Power and declared, "I have a Thin Power now and I'm not going to ever lose it again!"

Jean might have been known for her common touch but it did not extend to fat bodies. A letter reprinted in her column asserted that fat could be beautiful. "I must say, however, that I found it difficult to believe you really mean what you're saying," she wrote. "I don't think fat is beautiful, and I don't think many other people think so, either. Fat is anything but beautiful—the word itself is unattractive. Overweight people usually don't look good, don't move well, have a lot of health related problems, and don't, as a rule, feel as well as they're entitled to."

This was also the era when an alternative lifestyle to diet culture was slowly moving from the margins of society to the mainstream. A group of activists in the late 1960s was coming together under the banner of fat acceptance to fight the social stigma of being fat. While young people were gathering in urban parks for be-ins to protest the war in Vietnam, in 1967 fat activists were inspired to stage a "Fat-In" to fight weight discrimination. And so five hundred people—both fat and thin—congregated in Central Park, in New York, ate ice cream, and burned diet books and posters of Twiggy (who weighed around ninety pounds in her heyday). They carried signs saying BUDDHA WAS FAT and wore buttons that read HELP CURE EMACIATION and TAKE A FAT GIRL TO DINNER. One of the activists, Steve Post, told a reporter, "We want to show we feel happy, not guilty."

In 1967, Llewellyn "Lew" Louderback wrote an essay titled "More People Should Be Fat" that appeared in the *Saturday Evening Post;* it later became a book called *Fat Power.* "Fat, we are told, is ugly," he began. His argument was that fat people shouldn't try to become thin or maintain a thin weight, that they had a different body type that was virtually impossible to change, not to mention that dieting was bad for fat people's mental health. Fat people should no longer suffer by trying to pass as thin people. "American culture, for all its liberal ideas, seems intent on forcing a single acceptable form of body build on everyone," he wrote. In 1969, the National Association to Advance Fat Acceptance was founded by a biomedical engineer, Bill Fabrey, which he explained aimed "to make the world a safer and more pleasant place for persons of size, and for them to like themselves better, and lastly, and less important, for nobody to tell me what my taste should be."

Feminism and fat were intertwined because food and womanhood were intertwined. Feeding the household, cooking, and running the kitchen were all still the domain of women. Women's weight mattered more than men's— women were still valued in society for their looks over anything else. The idea that dieting could perhaps be more damaging to a woman than being fat was just starting to percolate.

Susie Orbach, a British psychologist, addressed these subjects in her 1978 book *Fat Is a Feminist Issue*. Orbach didn't tackle fat acceptance so much as why people used food as something beyond nourishment. She saw compulsive eating (but really, what is that phrase? One person's compulsion is another person's normal behavior) as an adaptation to sexist pressure in contemporary society, "as *both* a symptom and a problem in itself." Orbach wrote that we should surround ourselves with the food we crave so we can "go on with the business of living."

Orbach was not the only writer tackling the links between women's liberation, health, and weight. Some took a more radical approach. Writing in the *Liberation News Service*, Roberta Weintraub noted, "Fat is a defense against men...but it is a major source of conflict and unhappiness in women." It makes sense—if a woman's body is, in a patriarchal society, her primary asset, then how she cares for it and shapes it and how she compares it to other women's bodies are tied up in her own path to liberation. For example, the 1970 edition of the feminist health classic *Our Bodies, Ourselves* proclaimed, "We want to become physically healthy and strong and enduring, through exercise, proper eating, and training (like karate) and proud of ourselves, proud because we feel good ourselves, not because we look good for others."

Orbach went so far as to propose a loose alternative to Weight Watchers (which she dismissed as "an external scheme") and Overeaters Anonymous, suggesting women meet regularly to share their lives, sort of like the consciousness-raising groups that were popular then, as a way to challenge society's unreal expectations of women. She recommended eight women per group and a weekly meeting of two and a half hours, which seems like a very long time. Some of Orbach's writing took a psychological leap (fat as a symbolic rejection of the mother's role; women being afraid of being thin; "compulsive eating is an individual protest against the inequality of the sexes") or was just funny (she called cottage cheese "a methadone substitute"), but her true goal was acceptance and support, allowing that some women, despite all this knowledge, might wish to lose weight, and that was okay. But there was still an intrinsic promise, as in every diet, that your weight would stabilize after meeting with your group for six months or that you'd stop dieting and feel sane—that following this path would heal you.

Is Weight Watchers feminist? The corporation profits from gendered stigma, so the company's fundamental goal is financial growth rather than liberation. However, what Jean's vision had in common with Orbach's as well as consciousness-raising groups' was that it gave women a place to be heard. That was the key to Weight Watchers beyond the diet plan itself. Jean rose above her peers like Dr. Atkins and was a hero to her fans because she gave women space and community. Dieting had always been something for women to slog through alone, guided by the faceless faraway writers in women's magazines. Weight Watchers was, essentially, another private way women had of working to keep up with the labor of femininity. Those meetings Jean devised gave women a place to share the reality of their lives, even if it was comparing various brands of artificial sweetener. The idea that being a woman meant suffering in silence was slowly disappearing, replaced by the possibility of opening up and asking for help.

Jean never explicitly called herself a feminist, but she was surely living a life atypical of most women of the time. She formed a company back when her credit cards read "Mrs. Mortimer Nidetch" and had the audacity to think of herself as having value beyond the home. "I kept asking myself, Who am I? A wife? A mother? An entrepreneur? The head of a company?" she said. But the price of being an outlier in her generation was tension within her own family.

Jean the thin evangelist had a strange relationship to friendships and family, a patent distrust verging on paranoia. "Well-meaning friends are the scourge of the dieter," she said. "Sometimes the reasons they tempt you are not 100 percent pure and noble." Friends, in her worldview, were envious and constantly trying to deter a dieter's resolve. "You keep your eyes right where you want to go," Jean said. "All you have to do is keep saying no."

Weight watching was working for the whole Nidetch family. Marty lost seventy pounds on the program after a friend told him his bowling score would improve if he lost weight, and Jean's mother, Mae, lost fifty-seven pounds on Weight Watchers too. In her column Jean wrote that her son David had bad habits similar to hers but he lost weight for two reasons: girls and Weight Watchers. "David grew into a handsome, slim teenager and a very good-looking man, if I may say," Jean wrote. "I have permitted David to follow in my steps so he can learn that just as some people have blue eyes and others have brown eyes, some people have an uncontrollable desire for food, believing that it is their solace, comfort, reward, etc., while others will all their lives be as selective with what they eat as with what they wear." Her younger son, Richard, was born a natural weight watcher. "It is a wonder to my husband and me that we could have produced a child who simply doesn't like whipped cream!"

Despite the fact that her whole family was on the program and reaping the benefits of Weight Watchers' success, the Nidetches' situation was not a happy one. At least, Jean wasn't sure how she should feel. She loved being on the road, greeting fans, being treated like a star. The first ten years of Weight Watchers were so busy that Jean felt like she was on a treadmill, just doing her best to get to every appointment and make every flight. "I knew I was changing: I looked different, I was making money, I was wearing better clothes. In those days I was afraid I would forget where I came from. You see, I was meeting people who would forget—people who got thin and would say, 'I was never fat' or 'I carried my weight better than she does' or people who made money and said I always had money or don't you have a maid." Jean was adamant with herself that she not forget who she was, washing the kitchen floor at night after working all day or perching some-what precariously on her windowsill to wash the windows. She said, "I feel that if you remember your past you can enjoy your present. If you get thin, you must never forget that you are capable of getting fat again. You can't get obnoxious or unsympathetic to others with the same problem you once had." The past was a constant specter. She had trouble keep-ing old friends and started seeing a therapist who encouraged her to stop feeling like she was responsible for not only her family but everyone on Weight Watchers—she called that feeling "the mother of the world"—and remind herself that she was indeed still Jean Slutsky of Brooklyn, New York.

But her family had a far more complicated relationship to the present, meaning they had less interest in Jean's ambition and even the comfort her success could provide. While Mae, Jean's mother, had pictures of her daughter all over her house, even a framed frozen-fish package on which Jean appeared in an evening gown (she liked to go to the supermarket and point to the box and say, "That's my daughter!"), her actual daughter became something of an enigma to her. She was proud of her but also bewildered by her life and frightened she would end up alone. She didn't understand why Jean couldn't just quit and become a manicurist and be content to live a life more like her own mother's.

Even though Marty was an officer in the company and Jean had bought him a bus company to run (which failed because he preferred being a driver to managing), he was horrified at the fur coats and first-class flights and occasional security guards. "When is this going to be over?" he asked. "I liked you better when you sold eggs." "He didn't want to be with the new me. In other words, he liked me better when I was fat," Jean said. Marty missed having Jean as an eating companion. Her sons were teenagers, and, true to their age, they were wrapped up in their own worlds. In any case, Jean had already transformed. There was no going back. Why did they want her to live a small life? "I said to Marty: 'I know you're unhappy and I don't want you to be unhappy. But I am driven. I have to do this and I know you hate it...' When you do something exciting your family is afraid for you. But I was never afraid," she said.

In 1971, after twenty-four years of marriage, the Nidetches divorced. "Was our divorce my fault? Maybe, but who knows?" Jean asked herself. But was she even in much pain? This was her first real relationship, Marty was the father of her children and someone who'd loved her before she really loved herself. Maybe she had grieved the marriage in those turbulent last years before it officially ended and was ready to move on. She said she was, at least. "Why speculate about it? We divorced each other. Forget yesterday. It's only aggravation to try to rethink the past and wonder what might have been." She sold the apartment building in Queens for six times what she'd paid for it and packed up her worldly possessions to be taken across the country. In the fall of 1972, Jean moved to Brentwood, California, a single woman.

CHAPTER TWELVE

YOU'RE VISITING THE DARK SIDE

December 2017

I decided to go on a Weight Watchers cruise to the Caribbean. When I told my dad that I was going, he wasn't particularly interested until I told him room service was free. Then he began to free-associate a late-night order. "First I would ask for some warm mixed nuts," he said. "And then I'd see what kind of pie they have and get a fruit pie with some ice cream. And I think I would want a nice steak with roasted potatoes and a good salad and a couple martinis." My friends thought it was an odd choice of vacation. "That sounds like spending a vacation at a Holiday Inn," Vera said. She should know—she's been dragged along on lengthy multigenerational cruises by a family that loves nothing more. "You know how you're always the first person to jump in the water? It's going to drive you mad, having to stand several stories above the sea and only be able to stare down at it." But the opportunity to hang out with fellow Weight

Watchers—those obsessed with the program enough to want to vacation with it—was too tempting. Maybe it would help me stay on the plan or make friends in the meetings. At the very least, I would get a few days of sun.

So early one morning at the end of autumn, just as it was reaching freezing temperatures in New York, I flew to Miami and took a taxi to the cruise terminal to check in. My cabin wasn't quite ready yet, so I had a drink at a bar on the main deck, even though it was eleven o'clock in the morning. There were advertisements for the newly launched Cense, a lower-calorie sauvignon blanc created jointly by Weight Watchers and Truett Hurst Winery, just three points for a four-ounce glass instead of the standard four points for regular wine. I tried it, and it was fruity and zingy—not bad, but not good enough that I would buy it at home. There was a glass elevator that faced a sparkly staircase. Almost nothing had a right angle; the ship was furnished with softly curved chairs, sculptures, and pools. They looked like they were writhing. There was a cigar lounge with a blue and white ceiling and a jazz bar decorated entirely in shades of orange. It seemed like the kind of place where a Whitesnake video could be filmed.

There was a large Weight Watchers contingent, eight hundred or so of us, on board. We were fairly racially diverse, though age-wise we appeared to lean heavily toward middle age. We were just a quarter of the approximately twenty-five hundred guests on the massive ship. (A Weight Watchers executive and veteran cruiser on board said cruisers say *ship*, never *boat*, the way Weight Watchers say *lifestyle* and never *diet*.) There were special Weight Watchers areas of the buffet with point values, areas where we dieters could feel secure that we'd stay well within our points and get a lot of vegetables and whole grains. I didn't want to eat any of the Weight Watchers food, the mayo-less egg salad or plain veggie burgers for lunch or the endless soups from the sit-down-dinner menu. Maybe the other Weight Watchers cruisers were just more committed than I was, or maybe I was just tempted by the alternatives. There was a large selection of wood-fired pizzas at the buffet just a few feet from the Weight Watchers section. And the cruise company that owned the ship was Italian, so the pizza looked delicious. I hovered around it, remembering a story my college boyfriend used to tell me. His parents were hippies and had refused to buy a television when he was young until the neighbors reported that he kept standing in front of their window, peering into their living room to watch TV. That was me and the array of ever-changing slices: pepperoni, some kind of spicy sausage, margherita, and on and on. A woman in a yellow jumpsuit with a Weight Watchers name tag, which we wore so we could identify fellow cruise members, sidled up to me. "You're visiting the dark side," she whispered in my ear. We laughed. I blushed. I was caught. I grabbed a slice of marinara without cheese and she took a slice of pepperoni. We agreed we'd just track it, both thrilled. We weren't breaking the rules per se because you can eat anything on Weight Watchers. But that big slice of pizza was six points and I was probably underestimating. There was also the option for pizza delivery to our cabins. I wish I could say I didn't take that option. It all paired so well with the three-point wine.

Miriam had told me it was a big deal for a Weight Watchers leader to be chosen to go on the cruise, so I was cruising with the best of the best. At my onboard meeting, I listened to a leader from the suburbs of New York say that "issues are in the tissues." I still can't decide if she was referring to adipose tissue (or fat) or Kleenex. But the message was that we might cry after a week of delving deep. Or at least make some new friends while enjoying fruit kebabs and skinny margaritas. "You have permission to relax a little bit, permission to do what works for you this week. Look to the right, look to the left. These people are going to become family by the end of the week," she said. To my right was the woman who had caught me eating pizza. We high-fived.

There were several Weight Watchers ambassadors on the cruise, social media influencers for Weight Watchers, except they got paid only in T-shirts and getting to preview new programs and app updates. Even though they were varying degrees of fat to skinny, they were all pretty in an extremely manicured way, with elaborately blown-out hair and full makeup, each looking like a grown-up version of the most popular girl from high school. I overheard one of them saying she had brought her actual prom dress from senior year to wear on one of the formal nights. Even though the ambassadors had to pay their own way to be on the cruise, they got special reserved dinner seating at the front of the restaurant with the Weight Watchers executives and me. I wasn't there undercover—a Weight Watchers representative had told me the cruise was a good place to meet fellow members. I had taken to literally wearing old silk pajamas to dinner and had given up on my hair, wearing it in a messy bun all week long. Which is maybe the reason one of the ambassadors told me to leave the table. "Um, these seats are reserved," she explained to me. She was wearing a black ball gown and had flowing dark hair. Had I landed in the realm of the fat mean girl? Was I being told I couldn't sit with them because I was too dumpy for the cool fat kids? Sort of. "No, she's with us," one of the Weight Watchers executives said, defending my honor. And then the ambassador blushed. "I am so sorry for being such a bitch," she said. We laughed and hugged, and every time we ran into each other we'd affect sidelong glances, whisper, "These seats are reserved," and giggle. We disco-danced together one night after dinner when several members of the waitstaff did a dance to Donna Summer's "Hot Stuff" for no discernible reason.

I kept thinking of my favorite quote from David Foster Wallace's classic essay "Shipping Out: On the (Nearly Lethal) Comforts of a Luxury Cruise": "The promise is not that you *can* experience great pleasure but that you *will.*" I am, at heart, not someone who enjoys being forced to bond with strangers; I don't like to be forced to do anything. But I did make myself participate in group activities, like taking a yoga class outside on the top deck taught by a leader from Georgia who had the chipper and highly strung demeanor of a cheerleader. There were several ports to stop in—St. Thomas, St. Maarten—but they all had similar Tex-Mex chain restaurants and places to get souvenirs. We stopped in the Bahamas and I went snorkeling and then drank rum punch on a catamaran. I took a selfie while sailing, wearing a one-shoulder swimsuit, and thought I didn't look bad. At night I gossiped with the ambassadors at the piano lounge about the one South African deckhand who looked like an astronaut and whom even the married women tried to make small talk and flirt with. But I also caught a cold that was ravaging the ship and spent twenty-four hours in bed skipping aqua-cycling and Italian-inspired cooking classes, glad to have an excuse to read forgettable coming-of-age novels and look out over my tiny balcony to the churning sea below me. In these moments I would pretend I was just another passenger and not on an immersive diet-vacation.

I wouldn't say the other people on the cruise became family. In fact, I was relieved when we returned to Miami. It's hard for me to break out of my shell around strangers, let alone try to rely on them as a group. Even though members of Weight Watchers can participate solo without even setting foot in a physical location, the core of the company is still its meetings. The group aspect was just as essential, if not more, than eating liver once a week or weighing in. It was the heart of Jean's idea and still a large part of what makes Weight Watchers distinctive. The very act of sharing and listening turns dieting into an opportunity for growth, transformation, empowerment—all those things I thought I wanted. I wanted to get everything I could out of this experience, both on this cruise and at meetings at home in Brooklyn, but I kept coming up against my own ambivalence toward really devoting myself to Weight Watchers. The chief conflict was between my desire to do what was required and my awareness that my heart wasn't in it, really. I saw through the diet and past it.

Despite the pizza buffet, I managed to come home from the

cruise about three-quarters of a pound lighter. Miriam asked what non-food-related ways we used to deal with emotions and winding down. This was the kind of thing I instinctively shied away from talking about, so I listened as Patrice said she meditated every morning and Rosemarie said she watched trashy TV. I decided that some members liked the audience that Weight Watchers meetings provided. I just sat there on Sunday morning and listened, halfheartedly, the way I imagined some adolescents did when their parents forced them to attend Mass. The word *watching* in Weight Watchers implies surveillance. When I thought I hadn't lost weight, I skipped the meeting, even though it was perfectly acceptable to go without weighing in, and even if I weighed in and found I'd gained weight, no one would know but me.

I took a taxi home feeling frustrated with myself despite the weight loss. No one was forcing me to go to meetings. I took out my journal and wrote myself a pep talk about how I needed to work on just showing up and letting the program work for me. I had to open up, try to get to know my fellow Weight Watchers, let myself be vulnerable and feel corny in public—those should be some goals besides weight loss for the next few months. But it sounded like someone else's jargon in my head. Was I trying to make over my personality the way I wanted to make over my body? Once I got home, I put together an elaborate salad with roasted cauliflower, chopped endive, kidney beans, feta cheese, and a rosemary, lemon, and olive oil dressing. It was both delicious and Weight Watchers–friendly, but I was still unsatisfied, less with the food than with myself.

CHAPTER THIRTEEN

I'M A PUSHER

1973

On June 11, 1973, Weight Watchers celebrated its tenth anniversary with a sold-out crowd at Madison Square Garden. By that year there were 110 franchises and the company was making $15 million annually. Jean asked Howard Rubenstein, the legendary public relations guru whose agency worked with New York institutions like the Yankees and the New York Metropolitan Opera, to handle publicity for the anniversary party. His firm managed to get Times Square temporarily renamed Weight Watchers Square, which someone pointed out was better than Weight Watchers Round.

The celebrations kicked off the afternoon of June 10 with a seventieth birthday party for the TV host Bob Hope, who had become a friend of Jean's. An Australian who had lost 150 pounds presented Hope with a seven-foot-tall stuffed kangaroo that had been flown in from Sydney and then driven into Manhattan with its head and tail sticking out of a cab's windows. The party quickly became rollicking even though alcohol was still not permitted on the Weight Watchers program. *Laugh-In* comedian Ruth Buzzi, who had lost weight on the program, did a bump and grind on top of a table, announcing that Weight Watchers had made her a sex symbol. "Someone should build a statue of Jean," shouted the singer Pearl Bailey.

For the gala event, 16,500 devoted Weight Watchers members, including a group of 376 people who had come on three planes from Kansas City, crowded into the arena. Al Lippert appeared first, thanked everyone for coming, and introduced the radio DJ William B. Williams as master of ceremonies. Next up, Pearl Bailey came onstage and "sang and clowned and hoofed," according to a *Weight Watchers* magazine recap of the night. Then the composer and lyricist—and Weight Watchers member—Billy Barnes took the stage with Buzzi, the opera singer Roberta Peters, and the comedian Charles Nelson Reilly to sing satirical songs about what it was like to be thin having once been fat. Bob Hope, seemingly recovered from his birthday party the day before, entered next with a patter of jokes. "I once tried a waist cinch, but when I hooked the garter belt to my socks, it snapped my height down two feet," he said. Another gag was about his friend the actor Jackie Gleason. "He's constantly dieting. But the other day he slipped. He got off a plane in Miami and ate a catering truck." Reilly came out again and talked about his own success on the program and then announced, "I'm going to be *Weight Watchers* magazine's first centerfold." The crowd roared.

To thundering applause, Jean came onstage wearing an orchid-pink gown. Here was the main event everyone had been waiting for. "When I came out, all those thousands of people rose to their feet, clapping and shouting. I was like Cinderella to them. I was quite moved, as you might imagine, and asked for the lights to be brought up. I said I wanted to see all the beautiful people out there," she said. It was the culmination of it all. "My dear, dear friends. Tonight you have made me the happiest lady in the whole world," Jean began. She referred to herself as Saint Jean Slutsky of Brooklyn, New York, and talked about her humble beginnings, the growth of the company, and how thrilled she was at its present success. She invited twenty-one members who had lost incredible amounts of weight—4,000 pounds in total—to share the stage with her. One of them was a fifteen-year-old girl who had lost 203 pounds; she said through tears that the weight loss had turned her from an introvert who did nothing into someone who sang in the school show and gave speeches on the importance of weight loss. "I participate where before I was a sideliner," she said.

Jean talked for two hours. "I nearly drowned off a cruise ship off of Casablanca, it was hit by a tidal wave. All I could think about was how I turned down the peach flambé at dinner. Now that's appetite," she said. (This was a version of a joke she frequently made. Another, recounted by Charles Nelson Reilly, was "There was a terrible storm on a cruise ship and Jean said, 'Put the cake by me. If we're going down, I'm eating the cake and the ice cream.'")

But some of her stories that night were more poignant. One she liked to tell was that when she was a teenager she would cross a park every day while walking home from school. The mothers would sit around gossiping and the kids would be sitting in swings with their legs dangling, waiting to be pushed. Jean didn't like seeing them ignored and would go and push them for a while. "And soon they'd be pumping their legs, doing it themselves. That's what I am, that's what my role in life is: I'm a pusher." Just everyone wait, she said, for the next decade. This was just the beginning. The celebration was indeed a turning point in Jean's life, but not in the way she expected.

During the anniversary parties, Jean complained that the worst part of all the celebrating was being feted with cakes—small cakes, large cakes, cakes of every color and flavor, birthday cakes, and gigantic Weight Watchers anniversary cakes that were the largest of all. But Jean did what she always instructed dieters to do, which was to blow out the candles and serve it up and not eat a bite. She swore she never ate any.

But Jean also swore that she never gained any of the weight back, that the most she ever weighed after losing all the weight was 150 pounds in 1988 when she was sixty-five years old. That makes for an easy and enviable narrative of the woman who beat the odds and yet still woke up every morning to feel her body and make sure she wasn't fat. As if to underscore Jean's determination, in March 1972 *Weight Watchers* magazine ran a long story on handwriting analysis by Hilda Halpern, who looked at a sample of Jean's writing and found this: "Some hooks and knots on her letters accentuate the fact that she does not give up her objectives easily…She, of course, will not slide back into her old habits...Jean will keep her eye on the goal weight." Jean was the face of Weight Watchers, so it made sense from an image standpoint that her weight loss remain a perfect downward trajectory. But the truth was different. In reality her weight fluctuated. She gained weight when she quit smoking, then lost it, then gained weight again after she had a hysterectomy. In private, friends and colleagues struggled with what to do when Jean gained weight. She had many speaking engagements, and a twenty-pound gain was visible; tall with long legs and a short torso—apple-shaped—Jean would gain weight around her abdomen.

One of the reasons gaining weight feels like such a personal betrayal is that it can't be kept a secret. Whether it's something you want to acknowledge or not, people notice. That's where the shame comes in. It was no different in Jean's case. Her weight fluctuations were spoken about in hushed tones behind closed doors: "Jean's gained weight again." The paradox is that, in Weight Watchers, Jean cultivated a culture of dieters being in it together, and yet, at the end of the day, every dieter wages the same small war with herself.

What if Jean had been open about her struggles? What if the answer to how she managed to stay thin and not struggle with weight was that she did struggle all the time and was sometimes unsuccessful? Her charisma and gift as a public speaker would have only been heightened by such an admission. Acknowledging her flaws would have made her a more modern celebrity—in the Oprah vein—and her fans might have responded to her vulnerability. But I'm thinking like a person born in 1977, not 1923.

Jean's version was that everything was fine. She was loving life, dating the actor Glenn Ford and Fred Astaire, with whom she was photographed for the February 1973 issue of *Weight Watchers* magazine, even though she refused to dance. She played an astronaut's wife in a 1971 TV pilot that was never picked up as a series. Colgate asked her to do a commercial, but both she and Weight Watchers decided against having her endorse another company. At one point there was a TV movie about Jean's life in the works. She wanted Sharon Gless from *Cagney & Lacey* to play her. Her face appeared on a Mardi Gras doubloon the same year the shark from *Jaws* was on one. It's hard to tell if she was enjoying the freedom to branch out and experiment with her fame or if she was flailing. She wanted to try her hand at becoming a real celebrity like the actresses she loved and the men she dated. But it was an era before the celebrity talk-show host or bona fide lifestyle guru, and the entertainment industry didn't seem to know how to use her brash energy.

In 1975 she was dating an eye doctor who invited her on a three-month around-the-world cruise. She insisted that they stay in cabins on different decks. Within a week, she rather impetuously married another man, the bass player in the ship's band, Frank Schifano, whom she called her Italian stallion. The ship's captain officiated. When they got back to Los Angeles, they had a ceremony at her home. Schifano had once played in Rosemary Clooney's band, so Clooney came and sang "Come on-a My House" during the reception. "We never fought, but we never talked either," Jean said. She cut him a check and told him to go with God. They stayed together only a few months, but Jean and Frank never officially divorced.

In the winter of 1973, a few months before the tenth-anniversary celebrations, something else happened that Jean glossed over. At the annual meeting, she decided not to run for reelection as the director or president of Weight Watchers. Just ten years after founding her company she stepped down. She said she was tired of the constant travel and the demands of promotional appearances. Jean didn't want to just sit behind a desk; she wanted to be with the people, in the dieting trenches, where she could connect with them one-on-one. "In the end I wished them good health and said goodbye," she said. Those ten years had been relentless, and she could never have imagined how successful her company would become. She probably needed a break.

But that can't be the whole story. This was the woman, after all, who had optimistically added *International* to Weight Watchers official corporate papers before they had a single location, who claimed to love all the attention, and who delighted in special treatment. Back in the 1950s, when she bonded with a stranger on the beach in Florida over their stillbirths, she knew sharing her story helped. Weight Watchers meetings weren't just her life's work; they were her coping mechanism. Jean was only forty-nine years old, in good health, newly single, and with college-age sons. It seems unlikely to me that she left Weight Watchers entirely of her own accord. Jean was gradually of less and less use to an expanding empire. It was likely easier from a public relations standpoint to have her quietly step down from leadership and remain on as a neutered spokesperson rather than having her leave the company altogether. The role Jean was left to play was simply the Weight Watchers mascot.

CHAPTER FOURTEEN

THEY'LL ALL BE GONE BY VALENTINE'S DAY

January 2018

It was early January, which meant that Weight Watchers meetings would be packed with people hoping for a new beginning. Even though the Park Slope meeting was a friendly place, there was some snobbery among the regulars regarding the new people. "They'll all be gone by Valentine's Day," whispered Sadie, one of the Hasidic women. She had bright blue eyes and wore a light brown wig cut into a long shag and a Burberry trench to every meeting. I liked sitting near her because she muttered sarcastic comments throughout the meeting, things like "All men have to do is quit drinking and they lose ten pounds," which was what she said when a new member, a man who was a high-school teacher, introduced himself. "My mother sent me a page from some magazine of a woman who lost sixty-three pounds who is exactly my age and it was entitled 'How I Found My Feel-Great Weight,'" I told Sadie. "There was nothing else in the envelope, just that." "That sounds like the beginning of a horror movie," she said and we laughed until another new person shushed us. Sadie was trying to lose the weight she'd gained with the birth of her youngest daughter and went to three meetings a week, following Miriam to different locations around Brooklyn. I wondered if she felt the same tension and excitement about the mix of people at meetings that I did. I imagined that her life at home in Crown Heights, surrounded by Hasidic Jews, was very different from her Weight Watchers world—maybe that was why she came three days a week; it was an opportunity to interact with people who were unlike her in every way other than that they were also dealing with the same body issues. And I would have asked but I felt like there was a hard boundary there. We could smile and laugh a little about how many points were in a chocolate babka ("A zillion!" Sadie trills) on a Sunday morning but we'd probably never go for coffee after.

I hadn't weighed myself in almost a month, which I blamed on the holidays, during which I exercised almost every day but also, notably, spent nearly a hundred dollars on a Szechuan takeout order just for me. I also ate my favorite cake in the world, a chestnut-flavored bûche de Noël, which, apart from a slice I served Vera while we exchanged gifts before she went home to Maryland, I ate by myself. I was shocked when she left half a piece of the cake on her plate, and after she left, I ate the half she hadn't touched. Even so, I lost five pounds and then was immediately embarrassed at how proud of myself I felt.

I did own a scale of my own. I often moved it all around my bathroom and then into my kitchen to see if it changed my weight, as if I were going to weigh ten pounds less standing next to my kitchen table. Which was why this year I let myself be weighed only at Weight Watchers meetings; it was a way to contain my own worst instincts. Of course, there were Weight Watchers meetings everywhere. Royce told us with no small amount of triumph in his voice that when he was in Michigan to see his family for the holidays, he went to a meeting in a suburban Weight Watchers with his wife and son, who were both lifetime members. Miriam was also the kind of person who went to Weight Watchers meetings when she traveled. There was one she attended while on vacation in Hawaii, and once, on a road trip down the West Coast, she went to a meeting in Stanford, near the university. "It was very intellectually stimulating," she said in a sort of *Downton Abbey*–by-way-of-the-Bronx accent.

Diet companies have to reinvent themselves seemingly every January as a way to tantalize us all into thinking that their new plans will be easier and more effective than anything we've tried before. This year Weight Watchers was switching from its previous Beyond the Scale program to something called Freestyle. The overall strategy didn't change, but there was less food to track. Beans, peas, lentils, tofu, corn, all fish, fruit, vegetables, eggs, non-fat yogurt, and skinless turkey and chicken were all now zero points. The tradeoff was that you got fewer points to work with—while I once had close to forty points a day, I now had twenty-eight. "You tell a vegan that corn and beans are zero points and it's cause for celebration," Miriam said, looking visibly excited. "Think about it; you could go to Chipotle and get away with maybe six points."

Sadie glanced at me. "I don't see any challah here with zero points."

Jennifer had become obsessed with sending me screenshots from Weight Watchers Connect, the social media part of the company's app, especially the tag #firstday, where people posted unflattering photos of their current belly rolls or chafing thighs with captions like *I'm hoping this will be my first and last "before" picture.* It was maybe the most wholesome social media on the planet, where hundreds of people commented with variations on "You got this." Jennifer also liked to send me cringeworthy inspirational quotes, usually in rounded script (*Everything is #zeropoints if you don't eat it when you're not hungry*), and photos of bad haircuts, which, for some reason, people were always posting as a way of fishing for compliments. We were jerks, essentially, for feeling superior to these people who were putting themselves out there. But also, what we didn't say was that our texts to each other, even if they were done with a smirk, were a kind of motivation in themselves.

Jennifer and I are close to the same size, but otherwise I have never had fat friends. When I'm with Vera and almost anyone else I know, I am painfully aware I probably outweigh them by seventy pounds. There's jealousy there, sure, but I prefer to be surrounded by friends more beautiful and thinner than me; it's an ego boost, and they make me feel like I'm not as undesirable as I think I am. When I see groups of fat friends, I don't feel a twinge of envy. I've probably missed out on a lot of people who would understand the hardest parts of my own life but I feel self-conscious around fat people, constantly worried they will acknowledge my fatness and worried that traveling as a fat pack will make me feel the brunt of society's disgust even more. If I can ride along on the coattails of the thin and beautiful, I will.

One night I was walking to *Cruel Intentions: The Musical* to meet Vera. I was wearing a chunky cropped sweater and was all bundled up in a shearling coat and a giant scarf because it was well below freezing. I bumped into a woman on Bleecker Street as I was hurrying to the theater. I heard her say, "Big fat people take up the whole sidewalk." I was down twelve pounds! I thought I looked good and this anonymous woman I would never see again made me feel like I was the size of the sidewalk. Instead of thinking she was having a bad day or that the problem was hers, I took it as a sign that I was still a monster.

I hadn't seen Vera in over a month and hoped she might notice something different, an outside reinforcement to help me convince myself I was making progress. I was starting to get annoyed that my friends weren't noticing or commenting. I wanted them to tell me I looked good but I also didn't want to talk about my weight with them; I'm sure they felt awkward too. Maybe I was feeling especially needy after the incident on the sidewalk, but when Vera and I ordered cocktails—tequila and soda for me so as not to drink all my points—and she asked me about my "wellness journey," I couldn't tell if that was code for noticing I had lost weight or if she was trying to acknowledge that while I hadn't lost that much, I appeared to be making an effort. "Yeah, I mean..." I trailed off.

"I'm trying really hard." Here again was that ambivalence. Was I really trying that hard? And I knew I wanted her to notice something, but I wasn't sure what that meant. I left the theater feeling unsatisfied, like it was an off night for our friendship.

Most of my friends knew, or at least had a vague idea, that I was doing Weight Watchers. They had no doubt seen me order an unbelievable number of salads and noticed my social life largely revolved around workout dates with friends. If they brought up my weight loss, or even just my diet, it was a sort of tacit acknowledgment that I was fat, or had been fat, or was still sort of fat. It was odd that I thought I had thus far successfully hidden being fat or that I would have had to come out as fat to my friends. But I did follow a strange logic that if I didn't talk about it, maybe it meant my friends had never noticed I was fat in the first place, that I had successfully managed to hide in plain sight. These were the same people who often told me that I was brave and honest— words I heard often—for daring to write about my life and my body. Sometimes I wondered if what my friends and colleagues were implying was that I was brave to simply live in this body.

It was almost like a sick parlor game; I could take any compliment and warp it into a twisted commentary on my size. One Friday morning I went to my favorite SoulCycle instructor's last class before she moved to California. I was at a locker dressed in a sports bra and leggings—the same thing almost all the women there had on—and the woman next to me said, "You have such pretty skin with no stretch marks."

I laughed and said, "No, I definitely do." I made my way into class wondering if she thought I had given birth. Or did she mean I was lucky not to have stretch marks due to how fat I was? I wasn't even that offended—she was a fat woman about my age who clearly meant it as a compliment. A plastic surgeon I interviewed recently said, "You're so pretty," when I walked into his office. He was definitely trying to get in my good graces, but I've always been so desperate for compliments that I can recite every single one.

Who do we lose weight for? And who was I losing weight for? Was it just for me? Was it okay to want to be thinner to make dating easier? Did I want to lose weight so my parents would get off my back once and for all? I wasn't sure I had answers to these questions. Or at least, I struggled with my own ambivalence. Women who are trying to lose weight are congratulated for "doing something for themselves," while at the same time society imposes on them the assumption that weight loss is something done for others—in other words, that even what we do for ourselves is in a sense a performance, leading women to yearn not to perform, to own their bodies.

Dieting also makes you a bit of a narcissist. It's unavoidable. All that focusing so intently on yourself—your eating habits, the minute ways your body feels smaller or more taut, the cravings and guilt. Later that night after I got home from seeing Vera, I thought of an offhand comment she'd made about her husband being really involved in a new project and how she had to be supermom. She was looking thinner than usual, her sternum visible in a jumpsuit zipped low. So, yes, maybe Vera didn't understand the whole picture of what was going on with me, and maybe she wasn't noticing me the way I wished she would, and I was frustrated with her because of that. But what if dieting was also making me so inwardly focused that I wasn't seeing the things she wanted me to see?

CHAPTER FIFTEEN

LIVING OFF THE FAT OF THE LAND

1978

The absence of Jean Nidetch from the day-to-day operations was not hampering the success of Weight Watchers, which continued to grow, making it attractive to potential buyers. There were rumors of talks with Gillette in 1972 and then talks with Pillsbury in 1975, but the discussions all ended by mutual agreement.

At the same time, over in Pittsburgh, the H. J. Heinz Company was going through some changes of its own. It had its origins in selling horseradish and, of course, its famed ketchup in the late nineteenth century. For nearly one hundred years it was a family-run company with roots in the community and a paternal relationship to its employees. In the postwar period, CEO Jack Heinz, grandson of founder Henry J. Heinz, started to acquire companies like Ore-Ida and StarKist, of potato and tuna fame, respectively. Heinz was moving away from canning and into a more complicated product line. For example, frozen foods made sense to expand into because canning and freezing have synergy—a company that cans will also freeze—and by the late 1970s, they were good at it. The presumed next in line to run Heinz, Henry John Heinz III, decided to go into politics instead and went on to become a U.S. senator.

Enter Tony O'Reilly, a tall, handsome Irish former rugby player who, as the managing director of the Irish Sugar Company, had worked with Heinz in freeze-drying food. The company hired O'Reilly to run the UK subsidiary in 1969; he moved to Pittsburgh to work as senior vice president in 1971, then as COO and president in 1973, the first non–Heinz family member to have the job. O'Reilly saw the potential in Weight Watchers' frozen meals, artificial sweeteners, and bouillon cubes and agreed in February of 1978 to buy Food-ways National Inc., which created and marketed the line.

To finalize the deal, O'Reilly met with Al Lippert, who had trademarked the Weight Watchers name in as many places as possible and who had to approve any changes for licensing food products. The two men immediately hit it off. Lippert was a wit who often cracked jokes about the company, like "We're living off the fat of the land" and "We deserve to win the Nobelly Prize," and he found O'Reilly charismatic and a consummate joke teller as well. The meeting went on for longer than necessary. At some point O'Reilly got the idea that he didn't want to acquire just Weight Watchers' pack-aged foods but the whole company. Lippert told him that if he really meant it, he should call him in the morning. O'Reilly did and the two men checked in to a suite at the Plaza Hotel in Manhattan to work it out. On a Friday in May 1978, they put out an announcement, and by the end of the weekend, the deal was agreed on. H. J. Heinz Company would acquire Weight Watchers International for about $71 million. The deal was finalized that fall and Charles M. Berger, an advertising veteran who had come up with several successful Heinz campaigns, including "The slowest ketchup in the west," was appointed president and COO of Weight Watchers International. He reported to Lippert, who became Weight Watchers' chairman and chief executive officer, positions he would hold until 1981.

Heinz and its executives acted as elder siblings to their Weight Watchers counterparts; O'Reilly would go on to mentor one of the Lipperts' sons, Keith. O'Reilly and his wife, the Greek shipping heiress and horse breeder Chryss Goulandris, owned an estate in Ireland called Castlemartin. The Lipperts were frequent guests, and Florine Mark, the Weight Watchers franchise owner, was invited to stay. The Lipperts, who owned nearly six hundred thousand shares of the company between the two of them, received about $15 million, and Al Lippert took a place on the Heinz board of directors.

The Lipperts lived well; they had residences in Long Island, Manhattan, and Palm Beach. They donated to charity and ended up acquiring Weight Watchers franchises of their own in South Africa in the mid-1990s. In 1998, while on a trip there, Al suffered a stroke and died. Felice Lippert died of lung cancer in 2003 at the age of seventy-three. They're buried beside each other. His tombstone reads HE CHANGED THE SHAPE OF THE WORLD and hers reads SHE WAS HIS STRENGTH.

★ ★ ★

The Weight Watchers program was starting to become more expansive in a way that was straying further and further from the stringency of Jean's original plan. Partly, the company was trying to stay on top of and respond to a decade of odd and disparate food trends. For example, the nation's first salad bar debuted in 1971 not at a health-food emporium but at R. J. Grunts in Chicago, a singles restaurant. Americans spent less money on food than citizens of any other industrialized country in the world. Convenience foods like Hamburger Helper, the Egg McMuffin, and Famous Amos cookies all came out in the early part of the decade. On the West Coast, the pioneering Berkeley chef Alice Waters was fusing the health food beloved by the counterculture with a European farm-to-table approach to cooking at her restaurant, Chez Panisse. *New York* magazine said of the more ostentatious gourmet food trend on the East Coast, "Eating well is the best revenge." The *Washington Post* popularized the term *comfort food* in a reference to grits.

Weight Watchers responded in 1970 with its first pivot away from dieting and toward "eating management," with special plans tailored to issues like weight-loss plateaus and maintenance. In 1971 the company appointed its first medical director, W. Henry Sebrell, a former director of the National Institutes of Health, to keep the program up-to-date with the latest scientific findings. Weight Watchers finally addressed exercise, asking cardiologist Lenore Zohman to design an exercise plan that did not involve special equipment or clothes and that could be undertaken by anyone at any weight. She developed a program called Pepstep, which focused on walking and climbing stairs. The company sponsored a classroom campaign around nutrition education called "The Garden of Eating" that was commended by Congress in 1979 as "a model of socially responsible American business." *Weight Watchers* magazine, which had been published by Family Health since 1975, was getting five thousand requests a month for back issues.

It behooved Heinz to have a wider pantheon of products to sell, and at the same time, the food on the Weight Watchers program was expanded, partly because what was considered standard American food was changing. The palate of the dieter had thus changed too. People wanted variety— Mexican food and Chinese food—just as much as they craved hamburgers. For franchises around the world, the company made changes to meet international palates and cultures; the Finnish could have reindeer meat, Hawaiians could have poi, and Europeans on the Weight Watchers program could have wine before it was legal on the American version. The company stopped using *illegal* to refer to food off the program and started allowing much-requested popular foods, like peanut butter, popcorn, and small servings of wine, to show a small amount of flexibility. Liver was, to the delight of many, no longer mandatory.

At the time of the sale, the *New York Times* reported that Jean was "understood to hold somewhat less than 296,000 shares" in Weight Watchers and that after she relinquished the title of president, she had remained a full-time employee (as spokesperson) until six months before the sale and was now "active as a consultant to the company in charge of public relations." She received about $7 million in the sale, was not involved in the acquisition, and did not have a seat on any boards. Even her *Weight Watchers* magazine column shrank dramatically and stopped sounding like her. From the point of view of the Lipperts and Heinz, and on a purely corporate organizational level, Jean wasn't involved in the day-to-day of Weight Watchers; she was off in Los Angeles experimenting with other careers. Visitors to their East Coast headquarters didn't even think she had an office in the building.

I take a less charitable view of the sale of Weight Watchers. Jean was cut out, and there appeared to be a fair amount of sexism involved. Two male executives, deciding on a deal behind closed doors, didn't need or probably want Jean's opinion, and she didn't bring much to the table. "I know if Al [Lippert] thought that it was a good idea and that Heinz was right for the company, it would be the best course for all of us," she said. But the deal represented the boys' club that so many feminists railed against. The kind of people skills and charisma and command Jean had were hard to put a value on, so they weren't valued enough.

Jean Nidetch wasn't particularly savvy about money. She didn't even own the copyright on the Weight Watchers cookbooks or her own 1972 book, *The Memoir of a Successful Loser: The Story of Weight Watchers*. Even though she'd had a strong work ethic all along, she wasn't raised in a time when women took charge of their own finances. Years after the sale, she had no idea how much money she had made over her career. "It never really dawned on me. I still don't know how much I have in the bank," she said to a British journalist. Money wasn't what motivated her; attention was. "The adoration of the public is better than anything you can imagine. A billion times better than the money.

Sure, money helps to pay the rent. But the adoration! The envelopes," she said, referring to the fan mail and success stories that came in. Jean described herself as "wearing" the title of president of Weight Watchers International Inc. since it went public in 1968, which is a hands-off way to describe the role. "When we went public, we had commitment to stockholders in addition to members. I couldn't dissociate myself from the members for a million dollars or any amount of money, so I thought it would be better if I wasn't heavily involved in the business end of Weight Watchers."

For her part, Jean would say publicly only that "I was happy to be affiliated with a major company like Heinz that could bring us to even greater heights." But the changes to her original plan for Weight Watchers frustrated her. She saw the Heinz company making more foods legal in order to sell more of their own food and be friendlier to new users. She allowed her real feelings, for just a moment, to show through over a decade after the sale during a speech in the late 1980s while accepting the Horatio Alger Award. She was talking about fellow honoree Famous Amos founder Wallace Amos Jr. "I couldn't even eat those stupid cookies because it's against my philosophy," she said with a self-deprecating laugh. "My philosophy was changed by the purchase of my company by H. J. Heinz. They want you to eat everything, so we can now eat Wally's cookies." And then she continued talking about the fans, her real currency. By her eighties—thirty years later—she wasn't a millionaire any longer and said she wished she had saved more for her grandchildren.

CHAPTER SIXTEEN

HE BROKE THE SOCIAL CONTRACT

February 2018

I have been single for some time, and when I say "some time," I mean so long that I have acquaintances who have gotten married, divorced, remarried, and had two children since I last had a serious boyfriend. I know I'm certainly not the only woman who doesn't fit the accepted mold of what life "should" look like by the time you are forty—that is, married to an adoring man, effortlessly slim, the mother of two cute children, owner and mistress of a clean and stylish home, and upstanding member of the PTA. I tell myself that's not for me. The adoring man part sounds nice. At the very least, a good summer fling. But I am an unenthusiastic and inconsistent dater. I know there are people who claim to enjoy dating, just like I know there are people who claim to enjoy a cold shower in the morning.

There's inevitably a moment when I'm having drinks and making small talk with some man who I know I have no chemistry with when I start thinking about how long I have to keep up this charade before I can be home, eating ice cream and watching Netflix, reporting back to friends.

Every few months I'll have a moment of motivation and force myself to log onto whatever app or website friends tell me is the "good one" and sort through men. One Friday night I matched with an older man, almost as old as my parents, which was new for me—I'd always dated people almost exactly my age—but I thought of my mother and women's magazines that tell you to be open and so I responded to his message. I sent his profile to Jennifer, and it turned out he was a psychologist famous enough that she recognized him. He was a silver fox, I told myself, and was thrilled by his somewhat old-world mannerisms, like offering to send a car to my apartment to pick me up.

I thought it was a little odd when, after he answered the door and I said, "Hi, I'm Marisa," he said, "Yes. Yes, you are." What kind of bewildered greeting was that? As we sat on his couch drinking wine and talking about the use of psychedelic drugs in therapy, I felt like I was a character in a heady movie about mannered New Yorkers. It's so easy for me to fantasize when I meet someone and immediately begin to picture steps ahead into the future. Maybe this was the life I was waiting for. The psychologist and I had dinner at an Italian restaurant down the street from his apartment and he cried while talking about his teenage son. So sensitive, I thought, although he wasn't asking me very much about myself, and he let slip that he lied on his profile and was five years older than he'd said he was. He paid, we had another drink at his place, and he kissed my cheek goodbye. I was excited to see what might happen on another date. I wanted to get to know him.

The next morning, I received a text from him. It was not to make a plan to see each other again. Instead, it was a long message explaining why exactly he was left with a negative impression of me. The reason, he said, was that my on-line photos were too flattering, probably not up-to-date, and didn't fairly reveal what my body looked like in person. He was attracted to the girl in the photos, not the one who had shown up at his door. He used the word *deceit* and said that this was clearly an awkward topic but he thought I should know, for my own good. I was, in short, too fat for a second date. I ran a bath, ordered Indian food, and cried.

"It's like he broke the social contract," Jennifer said on the phone later that day after I'd given her the rundown on what had happened. "Men feel entitled to have anything come out of their mouths." I was glad she was angry on my behalf but I felt shattered, like he had taken the worst thing I had thought about myself and said it out loud. She said I had to write him back. I'm not that confrontational, and my usual philosophy is that not responding to someone is both the high road and probably maddening to him. But I wrote him back, saying first that I had blocked his number and profile so it wasn't worth trying to respond to me, then that, for some-one whose career was in mental health, he was cruel and awfully shallow. I ended it with *Enjoy your sense of entitlement.* That was the moment that made me believe my self-esteem could not withstand any further blows. I haven't been on a real date since.

When most women talk about other people and their

bodies, it's about romantic partners. One part of the body-positivity movement I have always resented is its adherents' repeated assurances of how hot their spouses find them, as if the only way to prove that you don't have to lose weight to be happy is to have a sexy husband who can't keep his hands off your "curves," today's preferred euphemism for *fat*. Loving myself more is not going to make the world treat me better.

I'm always aware of my body as a liability, so for every date who seems bored, guy I make out with who never texts me again, or man I meet who doesn't give me the time of day, I wonder if it's because of my body. In online dating, I wonder if I have a nice enough face to get my foot in the door, but when they see my stomach and my thighs they'll be disappointed. Including a full-body shot feels like selling an old couch online and having to include all the scrapes and tiny stains. Once, a couple years ago, I was waiting on a street corner to meet a guy from Tinder. For some reason, I can remember the exact outfit I was wearing: an Isabel Marant lavender-colored linen tee and a black cotton skirt. He never showed up or responded to my increasingly annoyed *Where are you?* messages. I should blame him and write him off as a flake or a jerk, but I secretly believe he came to meet me, saw me from far away, and turned around. Another potential online suitor inquired as to whether I was fat or "merely chubby"—evidently my picture didn't spell it out clearly enough. I know there are men out there who are specifically attracted to fat women—the chubby chasers, the boys who haunt Big Beautiful Women dating sites—but I have always resisted those men, even though I once had a psychoanalyst who thought that would solve all my problems. She also said, "Your face is perfectly good." But I wrote her off as very, very old, although well-meaning.

On apps and online I have ignored messages from men who lead with *Great curves* or *I bet you have a fat ass.* (And who said chivalry was dead!) I've never wanted to be the fat girl of someone's dreams—it feels both fetishistic and not connected to who I am or how I see myself. I find myself returning to wanting to be seen for me, not my body type. It's a brain twister of sorts. I want to be objectified, but in the right way; a miserable paradox.

The horrors, when I reflect on them, still feel endless. There was the guy who pawed at my belly while I was sitting on top of him naked and said with disbelief, "Look, I'm super turned on right now." The same man, who I always thought of as a nice guy, suggested I should begin dating black men, who would surely be crazy about the way I looked. For once I actually said something cutting in return, telling him exactly how racist he was being and how hurtful it was to give me suggestions on who might better appreciate me half an hour after we'd just had sex. Another man said, as he was undressing me, "I know you probably feel incredibly self-conscious about your body but I think you're beautiful." I believe he was trying to be nice but I felt ugly. A man I had been extremely casually seeing said, after we'd slept together three times, that he was thinking he should start charging me. "Do you think the only way I can get someone to have sex with me is by paying?" I asked, both yelling and crying at the same time. I did have sex with him later that night, but it's one of the most shameful things I have ever done, maybe a low point in how little respect I had for myself. At least I didn't pay him.

I haven't fallen for the dieter cliché of putting off my life until I lose weight. But the exception, if I'm being honest, is dating. I thought this Weight Watchers experiment would help on that front, that if I really applied myself to making my body fit standard norms, it would result in better dates. I am convinced dating will be better if I can be more content with the way I look. But how much are those two things really related? And what if I did lose enough weight to be able to attract someone who wouldn't have noticed me or wouldn't have been attracted to me before? I think I'm describing the plot of a bad romantic comedy but I would probably spend time obsessing over whether my love for my partner and his love for me were real if I didn't reveal the truth: that I hadn't always looked that way. Instead of the perennial thin woman living inside a fat one—an idea I reject—I would be the fat woman forever living inside a thin one. It is the flip side of my fear that someone will fetishize my large body and not like me for me. Even in my head, I never win.

If dating is the part of my life where I feel most like a failure, it can't be entirely because of my appearance. (Maybe some of it is my personality!) But my body has been the site of so many romantic disasters, so much, to use an overused word, *trauma,* I can't look at it as entirely separate. I want to be treated not just well, but like a human, which sometimes seems too much to ask. Especially because my body and dating life are not happening in a vacuum—as I'm attempting to change myself and my love life, it becomes public that women are experiencing systemic humiliation and assault at work. Time's Up and the #MeToo movement are focusing on show business, but the media industry I work in is affected as well. I have not been a target of harassment at work (although sometimes, in my darkest moments, I think it's because I am not desirable enough to harass), but I too have been experiencing years of disrespect of my body. I'm still trying to understand how that experience fits in.

"Assert Yourself!" read the cover of the Weight Watchers weekly pamphlet. One article described a couple trying to find a compromise between a woman's housework burden and her desire to exercise. "Describe the behavior you want changed. Example: You watch TV and I have to do the dishes after dinner so I don't have time to get in a walk." The relationship depicted was already making me feel glad I was single. "Explain the effect it's having on you: I end up not getting in my walk most days of the week. Specify what you want or need to change. Would you please do the dishes Monday, Wednesday, and Friday after dinner so that I can walk for 20 minutes? Clearly state the consequences for you. 'I'll be able to walk three more times than usual and it'll help me reach my FitPoints goal.'" I appreciated that Weight Watchers was taking a wider view of health, but all the emphasis on the individual, rather than larger societal change, seemed like only part of the story. Weight Watchers was a weight-loss company. It was not its job to make living in a fat body easier. In fact, it was good for business if people remained frustrated.

As I continued to lose weight—so slowly, just a tenth of a pound this week—I remembered something my mother had said about how addictive refusal can feel. I think she was talking about some chocolate protein shake she had made from a recipe by the makeup artist Bobbi Brown. Once my mother starts talking about helpful diet tricks, my vision blurs and I like to imagine my spirit walking five blocks away to the nearest McDonald's—a place my mom often mentions she hasn't been to since 1992, when I talked her into eating a Big Mac at the Del Monte Center. But her refusal made me wonder more about how it felt for me to be choosing the majority's side by losing weight. Status quo was wanting to lose weight and be thin. It wasn't radical, but was it okay to want it?

At the meeting, people weren't really following the cue to talk about being assertive but instead were in self-reflective moods, discussing their pasts. "My entire life I have been heavier. I was always the heaviest of my friends," Patrice said. "I had tried diets here and there when I was younger. I even went to a fat doctor where you got B_{12} injections and appetite suppressants. I lost fifteen pounds and then when I stopped, it came right back. That was me: off and on, off and on." Dieters love nothing more than talking with other dieters about diets they've tried and failed at, probably because they finally have an audience who understands. "I tried the Subway diet, the Atkins Diet, and nothing seemed to work," Royce said.

"I went to a doctor who said, 'We offer bariatric surgery and you're a candidate,'" said Rosemarie. People sort of gasped and whispered, "No," but I thought, *Sure. These days anyone who is more than twenty pounds overweight could probably find a doctor willing to give them weight-loss surgery.* Rosemarie's voice cracked and she dabbed at the corners of her eyes with a tissue. Miriam came over and put her hand on her shoulder. "I'm that fat you want me to get bariatric surgery? I'm not cutting myself open to lose weight." Rosemarie had gained weight gradually over four years working the night shift as a registered nurse. "I've always been chubby but never severely overweight or obese. I knew I gained weight. I was sleeping all day and eating all night. And I worked with a lot of different ethnicities, and everyone brought food to share for dinner every night and it was like a smorgasbord, a free-for-all."

I think what was unspoken among us was that even while Weight Watchers was currently working, we still hoped that we'd beat our own dismal records and lose all the weight and keep it off. There was so much fear about failing again.

CHAPTER SEVENTEEN

EAT, EAT—BUT NOT TOO MUCH

1982

Eventually, life in Los Angeles wasn't enough to keep Jean there. She had always maintained an apartment in Manhattan, and she moved back full-time in 1982 after spending a decade in LA. She decorated her new Fifth Avenue apartment with an egg motif (as a reminder of her early days as a door-to-door egg saleswoman) and came out with her own line of plus-size sewing patterns with the brand Claudia Cooper. The very 1980s designs made everyone look like a Nagel painting. Jean admitted she had been lonely on the West Coast, not for lack of casual friends but for lack of close relationships. "The pool, the house, the beauty of California, meant nothing to me," she said. "On the holidays I wanted to be in my mother's three-room apartment in Brooklyn with the rest of my family." Family was a strong idea in Jean's head but it seemed forever out of her grasp. She made great efforts to say to the press that she was moving back to town to be closer to her sons and young grandchildren. It seemed like she wanted to be the kind of family person that she wasn't, or possibly she wanted to have a different family, maybe one closer or less complicated than the one she had.

Weight Watchers opened up summer camps in the 1970s. In the March 1970 issue of *Weight Watchers* magazine, there was an advertisement announcing Weight Watchers summer camp for girls in the Berkshires on the shores of Rhoda Lake in West Copake, New York. Eventually there were several Weight Watchers–branded summer camps for kids ages ten to twenty-one and a few adult camps as well, almost all of which were co-ed. For a few years Weight Watchers also operated a spa in Northern California.

Campers could come for two, three, four, or seven weeks, at between $500 and $600 per week, and were tantalized by the possibility of losing dazzling amounts of weight, like eighteen pounds in a month. It was a fusion of typical camp and activities conducive to weight loss; some traditions (pancake breakfasts, s'mores) were omitted because they were not in line with the primary goal of transformation. As at most camps, there were two activities in the morning and three in the afternoon, but at Weight Watchers camp, end-of-day activities might be a session with a dietitian or an aerobics class. The company developed the menu and had to approve any changes, plus there was a dedicated Weight Watchers lecturer to oversee the kitchen and hold meetings. Initially the kids were supposed to eat the same plan as adults, but the counselors had a hard time getting children at summer camp to eat liver and fish, so they were phased out. There was a cooking studio dedicated to Felice Lippert where campers could learn to make healthy meals like roast beef with baked potatoes and broccoli. Dessert was often fruit, usually apples. Everyone was weighed once a week and lost an average of three to five pounds per week.

Jean started visiting the camps in the late 1970s, and everyone there and the staff made a big deal about the appearances going off without a hitch. The kids were even forced to do a dress rehearsal. Jean would arrive in a chauffeur-driven limousine and would ask for a changing room. The first few years, she'd dress up, but it was hot and it was camp, so she later showed up in pantsuits, which was her version of camp-casual. She would give a speech to the whole camp, usually motivational stuff about how important it was to get one's weight under control while still young. But this was Jean, a woman who claimed she felt more comfortable in front of five hundred people than alone and who loved an audience, even if it was just kids. It seemed like they loved her too. Afterward the kids crowded around her and asked questions. She made sure copies of her book were shipped before she came, and she would autograph them and pose for pictures with the kids. It was the highlight of the campers' summer. One year Jean's granddaughter Heather went to camp as a kind of publicity stunt and they covered it in *Weight Watchers* magazine.

The 1980s were a good time to be a diet company. The average weight of Americans started to rise around 1980. More than half of women worked outside the home by then, a fact that was blamed for the decline in home cooking and the increase in waist size. The expansion of Heinz and other companies like it created a huge industry of packaged and processed foods that Americans relied on more and more, as they did on fast food and takeout. Baby Boomers were becoming parents and the pressure for women to get the baby weight off helped fuel the fitness and dieting frenzy of the decade; by 1984, one-fifth of money spent on food went to diet food. Many of the same companies that sold high-calorie convenience foods began to introduce low-calorie and diet foods, such as Stouffer's Lean Cuisine, Diet Coke, sugar-free Jell-O, and Bud Light.

In aesthetic terms, glamour was big. Or, rather, glamour was about being skinny, which ran counter to the trend of Americans becoming larger—thin, which was always aspirational, was growing increasingly coveted and extreme. The *New York Times* quoted Ivana Trump telling a reporter, "It makes me feel powerful to be hungry." In his novel of eighties excess, *The Bonfire of the Vanities*, Tom Wolfe wrote of the social X-ray, the lady who lunches but doesn't consume much, her skinniness a manifestation of her soullessness. The thin and well-coiffed First Lady Nancy Reagan, a social X-ray if ever there was one, told *Weight Watchers* magazine she and President Ronald Reagan "plan our meals at home and choose moderate portions of fish, chicken, or lean meat with fresh vegetables and a salad of some kind. Occasionally, we have my husband's favorite dish, macaroni and cheese."

Fad diets abounded. In 1982, the *New York Times* wrote about the overwhelming overnight success (and possibly dubious claims) of *The I Love New York Diet*, a book coauthored by Bess Myerson, a former Miss America. Or one could try

Judy Mazel's *Beverly Hills Diet,* which focused on food combining and made such out-there claims as eating meat with potatoes caused the potatoes to ferment and turn to vodka in the stomach. She liked to say that she could peel and eat a mango while driving a stick shift and not get a splash on her white silk dress. Scarsdale, a wealthy suburb of New York City, had its own diet. So did Miami's South Beach.

Fitness, jogging, and Jazzercise (which Judi Sheppard Missett launched in the late 1970s) became ubiquitous, and maybe nothing symbolized the decade more than Jane Fonda's reinvention of herself in her forties as an exercise guru. First there was a bestselling exercise book and then, in 1982, the Oscar-winning actress released a VHS tape called *Jane Fonda's Workout* that sold more than seventeen million copies around the world. In it, Fonda wore a striped and belted leotard and leg warmers and exhorted her at-home followers to feel the burn to a soundtrack of songs by REO Speedwagon and Jimmy Buffett. "Whether you're fifteen or fifty, with the help of this album and a little hard work, you can achieve a well-proportioned healthy body—not to mention the outward glow that comes from feeling good inside," she said on the video. "So be in harmony with your age. Learn to understand and respect your body. It's your temple. And remember, discipline is liberation!"

Weight Watchers rolled out their own changes, allowing beer and offering a vegetarian plan in 1981. They launched a program in 1984 called Quick Start, designed to be more strict in the beginning for rapid weight loss within the first two weeks. It turned out to be a popular plan and Weight Watchers revenue doubled in two years. The magazine's tagline changed from "The Magazine for Attractive People" in 1975 to "More Than a Diet Magazine!" in 1985.

One Weight Watchers brand extension typical of the time was a talk show. According to one newspaper ad, the show teased "low-calorie recipes and high-calorie humor to sate your appetite." Also diet tips, exercising, makeovers. The half-hour *Weight Watchers Magazine Show* debuted on the Lifetime cable channel in September 1984 and was hosted by the British actress Lynn Redgrave, who had gotten an Oscar nomination in 1967 playing the chubby, plain, virginal lead in *Georgy Girl*. She became the brand's first celebrity spokesperson and lost thirty pounds with the program, calling herself "a thin person with a weight problem." In an interview on the Weight Watchers talk show, she said she was a typical third-born in her famous acting family. "I was the joking one and the amusing one and the chubby one. I became chubbier and more amusing to everyone excluding myself." Her parents were glamorous people who never dealt with weight problems, but weight was limiting to her. "It was so painful for me to be overweight. It was like a monster person lurking there who would overtake me," she said. "I was afraid I would lose my funny. I lost seventeen pounds in a spa and gained it back in two weeks."

The show was filmed in New York City and had segments on fitness, including how anyone could walk for exercise ("You can walk right out your door and start") and the benefits of water-based aerobics; how to order low-calorie food in a French restaurant; how to do a very heavy daytime-makeup makeover. There was a cooking demonstration for fresh fruit dipped in dark chocolate sweetened with artificial sweetener that was just 108 calories per serving. The program show-cased a lot of the company's own success stories, such as the man who lost eighty pounds and a woman who was an exchange student from South Africa who gained fifty pounds eating at Baskin-Robbins and lost it all.

One of the least expected additions to the show was the High-Heeled Women comedy troupe, who performed brief sketches around weight loss and body image. One showed a woman alone in her bedroom. "Vito, come on over, my husband has just gone to work," she whispers. Vito comes and he's a pizza-delivery man bearing an extra-large pepperoni pie. In another skit a woman stands dejected at a party and viewers can hear her inner monologue. Looking at a hunky guy, she says, "I'm fat, he knows I'm a pig," and she stuffs her face with pretzels. Another alternated excuses not to start a diet: "I can't, I'm Italian," "I can't, I'm on vacation," "I can't, I just bought a new wardrobe," "I can't, I have glands." The humor was poorly disguised self-hatred.

During this national diet craze, obesity rates increased from 12 to 14 percent pre-1980 to 22 to 25 percent by the late 1980s. There was no consensus on the reason. Some experts blamed low-fat or fat-free foods full of sugar, others corn syrup, still others processed foods. What they did know was that America wasn't getting any healthier.

The whole country was, in a sense, on Weight Watchers. Diet culture had evolved since the program began; Jean had not. She was a kind of living relic of another era of weight loss. After the tenth-anniversary celebration for Weight Watchers, in 1973, Howard Rubenstein, who had run public relations for the event, wrote Jean a note addressing her as "Cinderella! High Priestess! Evangelist! God-like!" He wrote, "Let's plan the next: The 20th—That one will have to be in the White House—at least—and possibly Mt. Olympus." Those words turned out not to be prophetic. Weight Watchers celebrated its twentieth anniversary, in 1983, with far less fanfare than it had at the Madison Square Garden celebration. The company threw a party at the Rainbow Room in New York City and plugged the ever-expanding universe of Weight Watchers products. Jean told everyone to "eat, eat—but not too much." Both the corporation and Weight Watchers dieters had moved on without Jean. And yet she held on. She was there to get a jolt of adoration out of the company.

CHAPTER EIGHTEEN

HEALTHY BUSYWORK

March 2018

My mother is the only person I know who can go to Europe for two months to celebrate her retirement and somehow manage to lose ten pounds. When she got back, she went on this Scandinavian-influenced diet kick where she ate spinach waffles that she bought from someone at a farmers' market and topped them with various kinds of jam. She called to tell me she received the lingonberry jam I'd sent her from a Swedish candy store in Manhattan. "I ate a spoonful straight from the jar as soon as I unwrapped it," she said. And then she cleared her throat and told me she didn't want me to worry, which is a frightening way to preface anything, but that she had to get her thyroid removed. "Why?" I asked. She said something about growths that looked malignant. I was talking to her on a street in SoHo and I started to get tunnel vision and thought I might pass out. I stopped walking. I could feel a lump forming in my throat. "You have cancer?" I asked. "We won't know until they take it out, but don't worry, it's the good kind," she said.

My mom has collected Mexican Day of the Dead art and mementos my whole life. In college she sent me a diorama of two people talking in hell that read, *Yes, but it's a dry heat*. It sits next to my kitchen sink to this day. That's what this conversation reminded me of. "They'll remove it but the damn thing weighs less than a pound. I was so excited I might lose some weight off of it." I told her I once got a full-body-imaging thing at a spa and learned that the entire weight of my bones and organs was something like four pounds. I'd thought they weighed at least sixty pounds. We both laughed. Then I told her I had gone to a Weight Watchers meeting that morning and found out that I had somehow managed to gain four-tenths of a pound even though I had spent the previous week doing, I thought, particularly well, eating salads and bland grain bowls I cooked myself and trying to resist the afternoon call to sweets. "Oh, I know. I ate four peanut butter malt balls and gained a pound," my mother said. Talking about food together felt like life was normal again.

I got off the phone and just stood in the middle of the sidewalk for a second repeating *It's the good kind* over and over in my head. My parents have always been healthier than me, my mom in particular, and even though they're now in their mid-sixties, I assume they'll be around a long time. It's easy for me to be angry at my parents, to resent them for their aggressively hands-off 1980s parenting style (with one notable exception), but I love them. My mother and I have the same dark sense of humor. Every Mother's Day I make a drawing or painting depicting myself killing her in some new and inventive way. We both think it's the funniest thing we can imagine, and it's probably therapeutic too.

She had the wisdom to take preteen me to see *Heathers* and *Hairspray* and *Dirty Dancing* in the theaters when they first came out, sensing they'd be important. She believed in having me take a day or two off every year from school for mental health and we'd go shopping and out to lunch. She gave me her copy of *The Secret History* to read after it came out, at the beginning of my sophomore year in high school. My parents encouraged me to write, sending me flowers and buying me earrings I still own when I had a piece of poetry published at age seven. They are everything, and, in a sense, my parents are all I have. I don't have a partner or children of my own; I don't have siblings; I don't have cousins who are my age that I'm close to or aunts and uncles I know well; all of my grandparents died relatively young. Without my parents, I would be truly alone in this world. It's something so hard for me to imagine that my instinct is to push the feelings away as soon as I can. I am not a crier; I want a whole lasagna or a pecan pie.

Without the coping mechanism of food, I searched for a different kind of oblivion. I walked half a block to the Louis Vuitton store and asked to try on a sweater I had seen in a magazine. It was the color of charcoal, a shade of gray almost black, oversize, made of a combination of silk and cotton. People say sweaters feel like a hug. This one did not; it felt more like a barrier between me and the world. I handed over a credit card I hoped had enough room on it and spent $950.

I believe people relate to food the same way they do to money. I certainly do—spending money gives me that same feeling of buildup and release, of temptation and transgression, as eating. I can obsess over the buildup, like a pair of sandals that are gorgeous but way too expensive that I visit every morning online, the same way I can spend days pleasurably thinking about whether I will order pizza on Friday night. I honestly don't know if my shopping is out of hand in much the same way that I can't really tell if the problem is simply that I eat too much food. I suspect I spend money as an easy reward.

But shopping is also a way for me to feel bad about myself and be treated poorly. Last winter I was on a work trip to Los Angeles, and, while killing time before a meeting, I went to the boutique of a French designer who makes clothes that probably look best on lanky women. I picked up a sweater and asked if they had a large, which prompted a salesman, unprovoked, to tell me in a condescending voice, "European designers don't often make clothes above a size eight." I knew that wasn't true, as I had plenty of size 12s and 14s from European designers in my closet, and besides, even if they didn't stock them, that sweater was oversize! I could feel my throat constricting and waited a second to gather myself. I took a deep breath, and instead of tears, I affected my snobbiest tone and said, "I *know* how sizing works. Do you have the sweater in a large or not?" He brought me a medium.

It didn't fit. I saw *Pretty Woman* for the first time as a seventh-grader when it originally came out. I know that famous shopping scene well—"Big mistake. Big. Huge!"—and that's not what happened. I'm not sure I'll ever get that scene where a horrible moment turns into triumph. Even if I had loved the sweater and bought it, I don't think there would have been a lesson in it for him. If I had come back a few hours later like Julia Roberts's character Vivian, armed with several overstuffed bags to show that I had money and style to make up for my size, it would have probably just made me feel sorry for myself.

Changing my self-image felt difficult enough, but trying to change it while getting external feedback that confirmed the worst things I believe about myself—that I was so fat as to be remarkable—felt impossible. I may be my own worst critic, but my critical view is reinforced and also shaped by society. How am I supposed to not hate myself, to rise above, when I'm so attuned to the cruelty of others? My parents in some ways were right—by failing to remain thin, I have failed at preventing my own pain. I know this isn't healthy thinking. But cabdrivers have broken their silence in traffic to tell me I'd be a lot prettier if I lost weight, a masseuse once told me while I was naked on her table that I should try going gluten-free, and an aesthetician said during a facial that she could do a lot more for me if I'd come back after I lost thirty pounds, and I find it impossible not to internalize these comments. So is the problem my own or theirs?

I can say that all this focus on appearance while I was on Weight Watchers kept me really busy—I filled my life with healthy busywork. I was chopping vegetables; I was riding the subway to yoga classes; I was spending forty-five minutes agonizing over whether I should order Chinese food or just roast some vegetables and have that for dinner. I was stalking women on Instagram who seemed to do a much better job at loving their fat bodies than I did; I was getting highlights to cover my gray hair; I was trying unsuccessfully to squeeze my thighs into vintage Levi's that had no stretch in them. I was doing so much. I wanted to be praised. I wanted things to feel different this time. I wanted my efforts to be rewarded. Except the best I could probably hope for was one of those stickers they gave out at the end of Weight Watchers meetings.

Once again I was hopeful for a weight loss. I was disappointed; I'd gained 2.8 pounds. My mom maybe had cancer, albeit "the good kind," and had to undergo surgery. When I asked her if she wanted me to fly out to be with her, she said that would cause her more anxiety. Despite all of that, I managed to eat salmon roasted with maple syrup and sriracha and lime from one of Gwyneth Paltrow's cookbooks and be the kind of person who orders just one sushi roll and eats a big salad to fill myself up. It wasn't fair. I know fairness is a fallacy, that it doesn't exist, but I was stuck. Why did some people succeed where others failed? It was a privilege to be able to spend so much time worrying about being fat. I enjoyed the ease that allowed me to latch onto a few big perceived failures. Life was pretty good when the scale had been the most enduring challenge.

For years I'd tried to ignore the pain by focusing on a

future where I wouldn't have problems with the way I look. But I was questioning how realistic that future self was. Instead of failing at dieting, maybe I was failing at seeing a realistic vision of myself in the world. Since I had managed to lose only fifteen pounds, the obvious was beginning to dawn on me: I was not losing Jean levels of weight. This realization was at once a disappointment and a relief. I didn't want the pressure of maintaining a large weight loss. Denial was never going to shape-shift into pleasure for me. But what if I embraced losing *some* weight? Why was it so hard to see weight loss in degrees of success rather than meeting a goal or failing?

This week's topic was diet fatigue. Miriam admitted even she had diet fatigue. "I'm trying to lose a few pounds and have been working out five times a week because I have my thirtieth high-school reunion soon and I want to have the best arms in my class." We clapped. She struck a Rosie the Riveter pose.

I had so far refused to make weird Weight Watchers recipes, which felt like the modern versions of things that would have been printed in the magazine in the 1960s, like these three-point "bagels" people at the meeting had been talking about. You mixed one cup of self-rising flour with one cup nonfat Greek yogurt, painted the "bagels" with egg wash, sprinkled them with everything-bagel season-ing, and baked. To this, Sadie hissed, "That is *not* a bagel." Nor was a "pancake" made with self-rising flour and non-fat Greek yogurt and a banana a pancake. I would rather have eaten just one fluffy blueberry pancake or half a real bagel. But who could do that? Certainly not me.

I wish there were an alternative, something besides completely eliminating that which tempts you or substituting for what you really want with something that only sort of resembles it. There is another philosophy toward food: having something rich but not overindulging. Moderation can definitely be taught, and I've done the elaborate dessert-eating exercises to prove it, but I am not entirely convinced I can learn it. There is a huge difference between food I enjoy and food that's good for me, although Weight Watchers would like us all to think that's not the case. Dieting is at odds with pleasure. A certain person—like my mother—can build a life around denying pleasure, but I can never exist in that mode for very long and be happy.

In the meeting, I sat in the back next to a woman I had never seen before who alternately ate cereal out of a plastic bowl she had brought from home and knit. She offered me a handful of cereal and I shook my head no.

Royce said he was bored of dieting too. "I'm tired of tracking everything, not eating freely," he said. "When I think this is forever, I feel a sense of despair."

The woman next to me stopped knitting, raised her hand, and said, "There's something going on in the cosmos, everyone is having a hard time and struggling." We all looked at her like she was an alien who'd just shown up to class. "Okay," Miriam said, dragging out the second syllable. "What can that tell us about how to go about our motivation?"

"Try not to look at it negatively. Say, 'I'm taking charge, leading myself into the better aisles of the grocery store.' It's like, if you enjoy bicycling, you're going to do it forever," Rosemarie said, always with a textbook-perfect answer. "Ease up. If you look at it as a second job, it won't work."

"But sometimes you want to be mindless and go back to the way it was before without all the weight," Royce said.

Miriam chimed in. "What about 'I get to' instead of 'I have to'? If you try to be one hundred percent perfect all the time, it will not work—that's where diet fatigue comes in because we're not allowing ourselves to have what we love. Think of it as the path to healthy instead of skinny. You have to use other measures of success."

So if I was supposed to look for "wins," as Weight Watchers called them, beyond the numbers on the scale, then there was this: for the first time in about a year, my white Rachel Comey jeans fit. Maybe *fit* wasn't strictly correct, but I could button the top button, and around ten pounds from now they would look good again. I was so hard on myself that I almost didn't count it. But I realized that was not the progress I was interested in any longer. Of course I wanted to lose weight, but at what cost? What I really wanted was to stop existing in a world where food was either punishment or reward. I couldn't disappear— I wouldn't—and, instead, I was resolutely living in the present, a place where, even if I was having a good day and concentrating on my wins, I was going to be reminded of my weight. There would always be someone who was all too willing to give me a whole bunch of advice I couldn't use and did not want. Could I find a way to exist in that world and be happy?

★ ★ ★

At home I watched Ashley Graham, the first real crossover plus-size model, give a TEDx Talk online called "Plus-Size? More Like My Size" that has been viewed nearly three million times. Graham stands onstage in a skintight blue dress and nude heels that show off her hourglass curves, looks into a full-length mirror, and says things like, "Thick thighs, you are just so sexy; you can't stop rubbing each other. That's all right. I'm gonna keep you." To back fat and cellulite, she pledges her love. As I watched, I smirked and thought, *Pretty sure she's wearing Spanx. Maybe a size 8?* (Later I met her personal trainer who swore that Ashley Graham was really a size 16 who knew how to pose to accentuate her naturally small waist.) Graham concludes by asking followers to hashtag their own self-affirmations on social media. "We need to work together to redefine the global vision of beauty," she says. "It starts with becoming your own role model."

Weight and the body have never been as widely discussed in culture as they are now. But I wonder if we've made any progress. When I interviewed Roxane Gay a few years ago, she said that, as someone who weighed around 450 pounds at the time, her goal was simply to walk through an airport without being pointed at. Have we made progress toward the right kinds of visibility? Graham is supposed to be an example of a larger model to make us feel like beauty standards are expanding, but her figure—flat stomach, nipped-in waist, ample bottom, great cleavage—is as unattainable and unrealistic and beautiful as Gisele Bündchen's. (I get a visceral reaction when anyone points to any woman with a large ass as being emblematic of real change in idealized bodies.) Almost no one in real life looks like Graham, just the way almost no one looks like Bündchen—Graham too won the genetic lottery, but why don't people talk about her that way? Why is Graham "accessible" but Bündchen is not? We are supposed to want her body but not quite as much as we want Bündchen's. It's not just a matter of weight; it's also a matter of body shape, the tyranny of standards of different proportions co-opted to be a strict set of regulations rather than a possibility. Part of the answer surely lies in why many people feel it is perfectly acceptable to point at a fat person in a public place like an airport. *Accessible* doesn't always mean something friendly, as in "I feel like I could go up and say hi to that person." *Accessible* also means that something is yours for the taking, both literally and figuratively. We should think more about the relationship between respect and accessibility.

Social media, particularly Instagram, allows me to follow attractive women who are larger than me as some token effort to reset my eye to a different standard of beauty. That app is the bane of my existence. For instance, in unflattering photos of myself I'm tagged in, instead of seeing how much I was enjoying a party, all I see are jowls and a short neck. Or the beautiful girls—who knew there were so many beautiful girls?—posing in bikinis or high-waisted denim jeans with no stretch encouraging all of us, no matter our weight, to embrace our curves, to shun diets, to just love our bodies—and, by extension, ourselves—already. It's all such a performance of loving yourself, of health, of fun, of flattering angles and good light and tight cropping. Even the fat women I do my best to follow have enviable bone structure and proportionate bodies and boyfriends with cute haircuts who worship them. And everywhere, women are talking about how important it is to love yourself and the body you're in. There is a well-known plus-size body activist I follow on social media. She'd lost a lot of weight in recent months but hadn't commented on it publicly. In an interview, she told me she was doing barre classes twice daily because she *just loved it so much*. It's possible that was the truth, but it's highly unlikely. I wonder what it would look like if she could be totally honest with her hundreds of thousands of boosters about whether she wanted to lose twenty pounds and what her real struggles were.

There is simply not much room for women to express any gray area about their bodies, and the internet hall of mirrors further complicates weight loss. How do you live online as a person unhappy with your weight? We are living in a cultural moment where fatness is a surface that denies interiority, fat acceptance is a further denial of this interiority—it is a way of brushing off the truth of living in a bigger body and just another performance for us of virtuousness. All of this love we're supposed to show for our physical selves is so dramatically oversimplified. We all deserve to feel good in our bodies and, yes, to love them. But as women, we are told that the source of our insecurity and our potential confidence is simply in our heads; we basically have to give ourselves something with one hand and take it away with the other. This new terrain where women are reassured that it is all in our heads is, in fact, a determined retreat from reality that is plain as day to see and understand. We essentially have to mediate the world's anger at us for our very existence. We're getting screwed coming and going—told to change our minds and set ourselves free, and then, once we feel a little empowered, we have the old hegemonic handcuffs slapped right back on our wrists.

CHAPTER NINETEEN

YES, SHE'S STILL THIN

1988

"Yes, she's still thin," read a *Newsday* story on Jean Nidetch timed to the twenty-fifth anniversary of Weight Watchers, in 1988. Maybe that was all anyone wanted to know about Jean, who was rapidly becoming a footnote in her own company's history. She had a perfunctory job title as a consultant to Weight Watchers, was trotted out to do things like be a judge for a Member of the Year contest. In this "where are they now" profile, Jean was happy to share that she worked out three times a week with an aerobics instructor who came to her apartment and that she stayed on the original Weight Watchers diet because it was easier than learning the new ones. She spoke about her life as if the work was over; her occasional interviews and speeches took on an elegiac tone of nostalgia for the work she had done rather than the present or future of her company or her life.

In 1989 she received a Horatio Alger Award, named for the writer of stories about impoverished boys rising above their circumstances. It is given annually to about a dozen Americans who demonstrate "personal initiative and perseverance, leadership and commitment to excellence, belief in the free-enterprise system and the importance of higher education, community service, and the vision and determination to achieve a better future." Fellow honorees were Truett Cathy, the founder of the fast-food chain Chick-fil-A, and Daniel K. Inouye, the U.S. senator from Hawaii. Jean was the only woman inducted that year.

Mary Kay Ash, the founder of Mary Kay Cosmetics, presented the award to Jean and noted that in Jean's time, women couldn't get loans on their own, but now, "women are recognized as having a brain, thank goodness." Jean, who wore a strapless black dress with tulle around the shoulders, joked that it was hard to slip the medal over her big hairdo. "*Distinguished* is a title I never aspired to. I just wanted to lose weight," she quipped. "I used to think that thin people had all the luck; they could eat anything they wanted. To me, being overweight was being unlucky. Today no one can say Jean Nidetch isn't lucky." She told the familiar story of how she had been a fat housewife with no formal education beyond high school who started a weight-loss group with just a few friends and now she had visited twenty-five countries on Weight Watchers' behalf and received keys to cities. It was her version of a stump speech, citing the 1973 tenth-anniversary celebration: "We learned to alter our eating habits and our lives change forever. With patience and determination we reached our goals and became, as one member put it to me, part of the human race." Jean was genuinely moved by the award, calling it the pinnacle of her work.

Many Horatio Alger Award honorees would return every year for the annual ceremony, and Jean met Maya Angelou, who was inducted in 1992. The author of *I Know Why the Caged Bird Sings* and Jean hit it off, so much so that "it was as if we were twin sisters separated at birth," Angelou wrote in her introduction to *The Jean Nidetch Story*, a repackaged version of *The Story of Weight Watchers*. "I liked her boldness and her sweetness, and she liked mine...If people feel comfortable enough to develop some courage, then they can do anything they really want to do—why, they can devise their own lives. What Jean had in mind was that she would liberate people so that they could develop their own courage and self-worth."

Weight Watchers was dealing with competition in the form of a low-fat fever that swept the United States in the 1990s, including SnackWell's, the fat-free chocolate cookies introduced in 1993 that inspired cultlike devotion and a lot of bad jokes about people eating whole packages; Baked Lay's potato chips; and the McLean Deluxe, a burger that McDonald's briefly sold. The Food Network, the first twenty-four-hour food channel, was introduced that same decade but none of its successful food personalities ever emphasized weight loss or healthy foods. Susan Powter, she of the shorn head and "Stop the insanity" infomercial whose diet advice was simply "Fat makes you fat" became a millionaire and a household name. Richard Simmons, the peppy aerobics teacher, had an infomercial for his Deal-a-Meal program in that same 1990s late-night-show heyday. Weight Watchers

International released its own thirty-minute infomercial, "A Brand New Woman," to set itself apart from fad diets. The message was "Health first, vanity second," but the info-mercial still sold a fairy tale of a woman who joins Weight Watchers, loses forty pounds, finds love, and eventually becomes an aerobics instructor.

Add to that the craze for the diet drug fen-phen, pre-scriptions for which were churned out at medical centers like California Medical Weight Loss Associates, which had sixteen offices in the LA area alone. It was so popular that in 1996, eighteen million prescriptions were written for the drug; it all came to an end in 1997 when a Mayo Clinic report found that twenty-four women taking fen-phen had developed a rare and serious heart-valve abnormality.

Weight Watchers could only benefit from the return to a drug-free and food- and exercise-focused approach to dieting once fen-phen was taken off the market. Without Jean as its public face, Weight Watchers focused on celebrity spokes-people. After Lynn Redgrave, there was Kathleen Sullivan, a broadcast journalist, and, in 1997, their biggest coup yet, Sarah "Fergie" Ferguson, the duchess of York, who had been ridiculed in the press for her fluctuating weight. Fergie an-nounced her new role as spokeswoman at a press conference at the Pierre Hotel in New York, describing a love of sausage rolls and her penchant for eating: "I am a regular woman with regular problems, hence why I am here today." Not that she was always the most relatable spokesperson. Ferguson published her own Weight Watchers–approved cookbook, *Dining with the Duchess,* in 1998. "At the first thought of doing a cookbook, I was skeptical, to say the least. First of all, I very rarely cook," she wrote, adding that when she was single, she mostly ate beans on toast, and when she lived in an apartment in Buckingham Palace with her husband, it didn't even have a kitchen. Now she employed a cook. There's a sort of cozy aspiration to her menu for "Writer's Respite," with ginger carrot soup, spinach salad with tangy orange dressing, crusty bread, vanilla-poached fruit, and a pot of tea. And "A Working Mother's Lunch," with gorgonzola and pear pizza at just five points per serving. The Highland Picnic was held—where else?—at the royal estate at Balmoral in Scotland.

For more earthbound dieting advice, in 1996 Weight Watchers published *Secrets for Success*, recommendations culled from leaders across the country. "I always keep a 'skinny' skirt or pants handy, which I try on often to see how far my weight loss has progressed. This way even if the scales don't show the pounds, I can still see I've lost inches. It really makes me feel better, and I'm more determined than ever to stay on my weight-loss program," wrote S.L.W. of Spring Hill, Florida. And "'I'm doing this for me'—is a powerful tool, far stronger than trying to lose weight for others or some special event. And once you have incorporated and learned to live with the basics, they're yours for life," from M.G. in Atlantis, Florida. It's probably solid advice but lacks the royal aplomb of Ferguson or the pizzazz of Jean's pronouncements.

As a consultant, Jean helped launch what would be the hugely popular 1-2-3 Success Plan, which introduced the idea of a points system and allowed more foods on the program as well as providing a way to keep track of them. One point was equal to fifty calories, as was six grams of fat. For every four grams of fiber you ate, you could subtract one point. (So instant oatmeal, for example, with 120 calories, two grams of fat, and three grams of fiber, would be approximately four points.) Crucially, 1-2-3 Success gave members a sense of control, a desire the culture seemed to require. An early 2000s article in *Elle* by Deanna Kizis explained, "The system is enticingly simple. Members calculate POINTS on their own, or look them up in the diet guides, which assign a POINT value for every food trend. Toasted eggplant crostini? One POINT. California roll? Three POINTS. Krispy Kreme original glazed doughnut? Five POINTS. A girl could spend hours tallying up POINTS for everything she puts in her mouth— it's fascinating, horrifying, and strangely exhilarating, like a scary movie you can't look away from."

Jean, meanwhile, was quietly going on with her life in a small but fabulous way in a penthouse in Manhattan overlooking Central Park. In her kitchen she had a wall of multiple stainless-steel refrigerators all filled with nothing but Weight Watchers food. She liked to shop during the day, going to FAO Schwarz for toys for her grandchildren, and had a standing weekly appointment to get her hair done at Louis Licari's salon. People would recognize her on the street and she would take time to stand there and talk with them about their shared commitment and how much weight they'd lost. She'd sign anything they had, like a movie star.

In the mid-1980s, Jean bought a unit at a condominium complex in Atlantic City called the Enclave. It was new and there wasn't a blow-dryer in her furnished place, so she called down to ask for one. Linda Evon, an employee of the building, brought her one and said she could keep it as long as she liked. Jean found out it was Evon's own blow-dryer; she kept thanking her and wouldn't drop it. The two became friends over the next few months. By that point, Jean's love of games had turned her into a pretty big and dedicated gambler in Las Vegas and Atlantic City. At first Evon didn't know anything about Jean other than that she was a high-roller who was tall and attractive for her age, dressed flashy, talked loudly, wore a lot of jewelry, and had a big blond bouffant. At the pool, Jean would point out a woman and say, "See that lady, she's lost a hundred and fifty pounds, she has a wetsuit on because she has loose skin." That's when Jean told Evon she had founded Weight Watchers and said she earned 10 percent of every franchise that opened. (Which sounds too good to be true.) She talked about her first husband who was a bus driver and about selling eggs door-to-door and that she used to weigh 214 pounds.

She invited Evon to stay with her in the New York City apartment. At night they'd go to dinner theaters off-Broadway, and the actors would come over to Jean after and tell her about their weight-loss attempts. She had lots of acquaintances like that, as well as longtime friends, many of whom she had met through Weight Watchers. She had a quick wit, but there was a sadness underneath it all—she admitted that she missed Marty, with whom she remained close after their divorce. He remarried and moved to Miami, where he lived until his death, in 2003.

"Come with me, I have a couple of mink coats I have to pick up in the garment district," she told Evon. "I want you to make this one into a bomber jacket," she told the furrier, who said he didn't want to cut up a perfectly beautiful black mink, and besides, she already had a mink bomber. "Hey, do you want to buy a mink coat?" Jean asked Evon. She offered her a deal of $700 for the coat and said she could pay it off in weekly installments. Evon agreed. It was her first fur and Jean's name was sewn onto the label. Evon diligently mailed her payments. Once she was a week late and Jean wrote her a note reminding her that if she was going to do something, she'd better do it. That's how she saw the world.

CHAPTER TWENTY

AN INHERENT DISTRUST
OF GURUS

April 2018

I went to Thailand to cruise around the Andaman Sea on a forty-foot boat for a story on wellness travel. There were eight of us on board, including the captain, a chef, and a trainer from a private boxing gym in SoHo whose $500-an-hour staff members were known for working with all the Victoria's Secret Angels. I spent a lot of time observing the trainer for clues about my own life, specifically to see if there was joy to be found in the slog of writing down and totaling the points value of everything I ate. Her body was perhaps the most beautiful woman's body I'd ever seen—and she had many tiny thong bikinis, so I saw a lot of it—with a completely flat stomach, a large, round butt, healthy thighs, chiseled arms, and not a single dimple of cellulite anywhere. The overall effect was that she looked expensive and high-maintenance. Her body wasn't just the result of interval training with six different varieties of burpees she led us through every morning but also the meticulous way she ate. The trainer talked about eating rice as "cheating" and was constantly drinking protein shakes. She had gone all in, and that total submission to fitness had paid off aesthetically. I think I understood then that having a body like hers was akin to driving a race car or having expensively blown-out hair or owning a rare breed of tropical bird—it's not easily sustainable and its care and maintenance basically take over your entire life. The perfect body is something we're supposed to be constantly working toward even when getting it and keeping it are impossible. We're set up for failure by being conditioned to desire it.

Our chef cooked unbelievable food, not just unbelievable as a slangy synonym for tasting good but unbelievable because the herb salads and curried soups and spicy grilled prawns and mangoes with porridge were also healthy. Between the sun and all the vegetables I was eating and the daily workouts, I was feeling like my best self. That is, until I asked Vashti, a tall, willowy fellow passenger—once again I outweighed everyone on the boat by probably seventy-five pounds—to take a picture of me treading water in the ocean. I was wearing my newest swimsuit, a black one-piece with wide straps purchased two days before I left on the trip. In the photo I looked pale and like I had no neck, my eyes squinty like they were getting swallowed by the fat on my face. I spent the rest of the week literally jumping off the boat and into the ocean to get out of the way of everyone's camera and volunteering to take group photos not because I'm good at it or have a generous spirit but because I didn't want visual records of myself in a bathing suit.

Vashti was newly single, and one morning after breakfast, we were sitting on the trampoline, in the netted part of our catamaran, talking about her dating life in Minneapolis. She said, "I'm just having fun." I wanted to ask her to explain what she meant. Girls like me don't have fun dating. She kept asking me if friends tried to set me up or if I was online dating. I continually brushed her off. "I'm working on myself," I said, which was true enough, but what I really wanted to say was that I'd rather marry the massive pink, iridescent jellyfish that had just floated past us than any guy I'd met in a long time. Toward the end of the trip we had cocktails at sunset on another boat, named *Not @ Work,* helmed by sexy pirate-looking men from England. I felt the electric twinge of being around people more attractive than me. I wanted them to want me but it never even occurred to me that it might happen. And none of them gave me a single glance.

Seemingly everyone on the boat had brought along self-help books to read. Perhaps I shouldn't have been surprised that the kind of people who would pay $3,000 for a week on a wellness adventure would be interested in self-improvement, but I assumed that this group of beautiful, financially sound, athletic, thin women had their lives together enough that they were beyond pop psychology. But what women say and what is actually happening in their lives are often two very different things, and their reading choices gave me some insight into what they might be dealing with. I picked up one book that asked me if I was the badass heroine of my own story. Another was from a self-described food therapist who categorized eaters into various types. I read a few pages and took a quiz and found that I was, according to the author's analysis of various personality and eating types, someone who ate lavishly due to fear of the mundane, which was accurate. But the book's solutions involved so-called clean eating. Orthorexia is truly the malady of today's bourgeois woman, what hysteria and fainting spells were to the Victorians. I bet I was the only person on the cruise who, on the way home, at a layover in Frankfurt, ate at Burger King.

These days the word *diet* is out of fashion; we cleanse, we eat clean, we are healthy and well. We practice wellness and self-care and they're part of our everyday vernacular. Wellness purports to be health for health's sake, divorced from vanity. It is really the marriage of diet culture and body-love culture made commercial; capitalism is at the heart of wellness culture. Wellness has become an excuse for doing what was once considered superficial; under the banner of wellness, the same activities are important, necessary, maybe transformative. It's all the times I have gleefully paid for wild sockeye salmon to top a quinoa bowl or justified multiple forty-dollar Pilates sessions or paid someone to give me a crystal healing. I've tried colonics and infrared saunas in the pursuit of weight loss. Anytime I write about dieting, I get a deluge of advice from well-intentioned strangers instructing me to try various life-changing tricks: go on the Lyn-Genet plan (already tried it) or go vegan (tried it) or quit sugar (tried it and lasted two days) or stop eating takeout (impossible) or check out the Beck Diet Solution (tried it). I was even offered a two-week stay at no cost at a Nutritarian (they advocate what amounts to eating a large salad as the main dish at every meal) clinic in Boca Raton. They all boil down to some manner of dieting. I have an inherent distrust of gurus who promise a new start or a quick fix. With my job, I meet people almost daily who have everything figured out. I feel that pull. I would love to just start doing Tracy Anderson's ninety-minute workout six days a week (which sounds like a part-time job in itself), as she advises her devotees, or go gluten-free or pay for my Transcendental Meditation mantra and realize that was all it took for everything else to click into place.

I can trace my participation in all of these out-there modalities to my early weight problem. Because I had spent my childhood eating organic foods and being sent to acupuncturists, all in service of lowering my weight, I became a go-to writer to cover those things in my adult life; they were relatively normal to me. Assigning me the story meant I wouldn't automatically write off energy cleansing or aromatherapy as weird. I owe some of my career to wellness. And much of what falls under the umbrella of wellness is fun and indulgent and things I would do even if it weren't my job. I go to Sky Ting, my yoga studio, so often that I've inserted myself into the lives of my teachers and made a whole group of friends there. I am that annoying person who comes into class and hugs a half dozen people and spends birthdays at retreats.

Two friends I've gotten to know from yoga, Lauren and Marisa, both former professional dancers, teach a modern-dance class called Moves that meets a couple times a month in Tribeca. I would see friends posting videos of themselves doing the dances, which looked like Kate Bush had choreographed a sexy '90s R&B video. I was always hesitant to go because I felt like I wasn't a good enough dancer and, honestly, because I would be by far the fattest person in the room. "Don't worry about it," my friend Krissy, a regular, said to me. "If you forget something, just flip your hair or do a body roll."

Right before the spring holidays, after I had spent a week balefully tracking the points of chocolate mini-eggs and egg-shaped Reese's, I finally worked up the courage to go to Moves. The space looked absurdly professional; in the hallways outside the studios, dancers stretched and chatted with friends. I felt like a bewildered extra in the movie *Fame*. But something happened once the studio door opened and several dozen of us streamed into the class: I let myself just enjoy being there for ninety minutes. I was definitely the fattest, maybe the oldest, and also quite possibly the worst dancer there. But as soon as we started learning slinky choreography to a Rihanna remix, I gyrated my hips and waved my arms and writhed on the floor like I was doing air sex. None of it mattered; I loved it. For a few hours, my body and I could have a détente. Did I look thin when I caught my reflection in the mirror as I spun and sashayed? No, not at all, but I didn't look like a monster either. In fact, I looked happy.

We are, culturally, trying to ride the wellness wave, and it is fun and has made my life better, but we need to look squarely at what we think we are doing. It costs a lot of money to participate in this contemporary iteration of wellness culture, even if it's just to dip a toe in it. My job pays for me to have these experiences but I certainly buy my own massages and body scrubs and yoga retreats in Italy, a pale version of what many friends and readers do, which is to seek out the often expensive treatments I write about. I am well groomed and scrubbed clean and smell good a lot of the time, which is also enough for a lot of people who know me to overlook the fact that I might have real problems. And I can understand the rise of wellness as a correction for women who don't feel like their doctors are listening to them or who need it as an outlet for anxiety. Is going to a sound bath hurting anyone? No, and a group sound meditation is a nice change from a big dinner with lots of wine. Wellness says so much about our current fears in contemporary society and, since it's so targeted to women, our shared fears—women's fears and the fears we have about women. We want to show off all the work we're putting into our bodies and get credit for it and feel that it's not for naught, that there's some higher purpose beyond mere vanity. Wellness shows us a path to excellence, but sometimes it's just a dead end.

Weight Watchers has also tried to benefit from wellness, even if a weight-loss company that formerly traded in artificial sweeteners seems like a strange fit. In early 2015, Weight Watchers was in its fourth year of decline in new members. It should have been the busiest time of the year for the company, so they decided to look inward. What they realized was that they were still associated with the Jean era. Diets seemed restricted, outdated, and definitely not cool. Health was perhaps trendier than it had been since the aerobics-led craze of the 1980s, but instead of dieting being the focus, it was about wellness, eating clean, being active, staying fit. Weight Watchers wasn't doing a very good job of reflecting that worldview.

So instead of hiring any other celebrity spokesperson, they approached America's most famous yo-yo dieter: Oprah

Winfrey, who had dieted very publicly for years. She'd lost sixty-seven pounds on a liquid diet in 1988 and wheeled a wagon full of animal fat onstage to her talk show as proof, wearing blue jeans, a black turtleneck, and a chunky belt. The episode was called "Diet Dreams Come True." The message then was that despite all Oprah's success, weight had kept her back and now she could soar. Except that didn't happen. She regained the weight and told *People* magazine in 1991, "I thought I was cured. And that's just not true. You have to find a way to live in the world with food." In 1993, she was back up to 222 pounds and began training with Bob Greene, and by 1994 she had slimmed down again and ran a marathon in four hours, twenty-nine minutes, and twenty seconds. In 2002, she wrote an essay for her own *O* magazine titled "What I Know for Sure About Making Peace with My Body": "I sat up in bed one crisp, sunny morning and made a vow to love my heart. To treat it with respect. To feed and nurture it. To work it out and then let it rest." By 2009 the cover of *O* showed a lean Oprah from 2005 alongside the current Oprah with the question *How did I let this happen again?* She saw her weight as a gate she had to pass through to have the life that she wanted. But if Oprah Winfrey didn't have the life that she wanted, what hope was there for the rest of us?

Weight Watchers approached Winfrey in 2015. It wasn't the first time they had asked her to be a spokesperson, but she was healing from a broken ankle and had gained weight, and this time she said yes. Winfrey bought a 10 percent stake in the company, worth $43 million. By late 2015, membership had jumped to 3.6 million. Winfrey also became the star of an ad campaign advertising her own forty-pound weight loss and her excitement about eating bread every day. By joining and being the face of the company, Winfrey had more than doubled her investment. Concerned fans and feminists alike wondered if this was proof that Oprah's ethos to love yourself and live your best life was just a façade, that if she couldn't get herself to self-acceptance, no one else could.

In April 2017, Weight Watchers named Mindy Grossman president and CEO. Grossman is from Long Island and calls to mind Jean more than a little bit. Not just in her platinum hair and penchant for a little flash in her clothing—Gucci heels are a favorite—but also because she's opinionated and direct and funny in the way Jean was. She's a veteran Weight Watchers dieter too. She joined Weight Watchers with her mother in 1971 to lose weight from her teenage frame, which was "a little chunky." When I met her, she raved about recipes she'd tried, a four-point shrimp and grits made with nonfat Greek yogurt and a zero-point clambake with lobster, salmon, clams, grilled corn, and beets. "Then I had people over and said, 'You know you just had zero points?' And fruit for dessert." She said the challenge for Weight Watchers was not a specific diet company or a book. "Our competition is people thinking they can get healthy themselves." That reminded me of a quote from Lorne Michaels, producer of *Saturday Night Live*. When someone asked, "Who's your competition?" he said, "Going to bed early on a Saturday night."

Grossman's mandate has been to stay the kinder, gentler, Oprah-approved wellness course. She described the current state of Weight Watchers to me this way: "We are not determining what healthy means to you. We are not determining how much you should weigh. We are not determining any of that. We're trying to give you the education and the inspiration and the tools so you can make that decision for yourself and make the right choices. That's a lot more empowering to people than saying, 'We're telling you what not to do.'" The very idea of goal setting was changing. I also interviewed Gary Foster, Weight Watchers' chief of science, who said that, ideally, people should take a break after every twenty-five or so pounds to reevaluate. "Nobody ever wants to do this. Most people are like, 'Just get me to my goal, we can talk about maintenance later,' but how big of a lifestyle change was it to lose twenty-five pounds? Those changes will get more significant to lose fifty," he said. "It's what the consequence of that weight brings in terms of impaired quality of life. Those are the things we want people to focus in on, like shortness of breath when walking up stairs. And it's much more meaningful than 'I've got to get to a certain weight.'"

In late 2018, Grossman led the company to rebrand itself, eschewing the name Weight Watchers altogether and going by WW (which staffers in its New York City headquarters pronounce "dub-dub"). The corporate motto was changed to "Wellness That Works." Instead of going to Weight Watchers stores, dieters attend meetings at a WW studio, and meetings are now workshops led by wellness coaches. A planned line of branded food will be "clean," with no artificial sweeteners, colors, flavors, or preservatives. The company partnered with the meditation app Headspace to offer members short meditations, like "Engage Your Senses When Eating" ("Take a moment to consider or appreciate where that food has come from, perhaps how long it took to grow or how long it took to make, connecting with the journey of that food"). Members can track their food and fitness with a new program called WellnessWins and rack up reward points for things like meals tracking, meeting attendance, and activity. Customers can redeem their Wins for various tiers of prizes, sort of like using tickets won at Skee-Ball at a county fair for a stuffed bear. The rewards are WW-branded merchandise, like a WHAT'S YOUR WHY cap or a yoga mat that reads POSITIVE VIBES ONLY, or products from partners, like a trial subscription to Rent the Runway, a fifteen-dollar gift card to Kohl's department store, or a vial of face and body oil from Nyakio.

WW wellness comes in a pastel-colored, euphemistic package, and while *weight* has been dropped from the name, in a statement, Grossman said, "We will always have the best weight-loss program on the planet, but now we're putting our decades of experience in behavior change to work for an even greater mission. We are becoming the world's partner in wellness. No matter what your goal is—to lose weight, eat healthier, move more, develop a positive mind-set, or all of the above—we will bring you science-based solutions that fit into your life." In an interview she put it to me more bluntly: "We are very aware when I talk about the paradox of health today that everybody's talking about health and wellness, and everybody's talking about the size of the wellness economy, three point seven trillion and growing. Nobody likes to use the world *diet* and every private equity fund is listening and we're getting unhealthier by the minute."

* * *

Back at my Weight Watchers meeting in Brooklyn, I weighed in and found I'd lost 2.2 pounds. "I know I gained," said Patrice to all three dozen of us as she walked into the meeting on Sunday a few minutes late and sat down next to me. She was in what for her was a bad mood: more defeatist than usual. "It's the beginning of my downward spiral." I made a mental note not to tell her I'd lost weight while traveling, even though I was sure she would have been happy for me. Miriam attempted to talk her down. "Our lives are not sturdy, they're like this"—and she made an up-and-down motion like a roller coaster with her hand. "I went to a conference and had two weeks of eating everything. Everything," Patrice said. "And then my stomach was bothering me and now I'm eating salad and soup for lunch every day for a while."

"It's a medicinal thing," Miriam said. "A parent-kid thing. The kid wants, and the adult says, 'Does this make sense?'"

"The thing is, you came to the meeting," Rosemarie said. Sadie, who was sitting on my other side, whispered to me that that was easy for her to say; she kept losing weight and was almost at her goal.

"I did come to the meeting," Patrice said and crossed her arms like a petulant child. "But I'm not weighing myself this week."

"Eat What You Want" was the theme of this week's handout, which had a picture of french fries on the cover. A childhood of dining at a vegetarian fast-food establishment called McDharma's and eating Brahma Burgers taught me to recognize healthy makeovers of comfort food and I remain unconvinced by these imitations. Inside there was a profile of a woman named Kelly from San Diego who'd lost weight on her fourth time at Weight Watchers. She was wearing purple leggings and a pink tank and standing atop a canyon. Kelly boasted that she made her own eight-point version of Del Taco's chili cheddar fries. "Friday I'm making pizza, and Saturday is date night." I have a natural aversion to people who use the term *date night,* and I in no way believed her low-point chili cheese fries were delicious.

But it occurred to me that this was my natural defense when confronted with people different from me: I looked down on them. I took the details I found tacky and wrinkled my nose, rolled my eyes, and used it as an excuse not to learn from or even listen to what they might have to say. I was a snob. Maybe apart from the weight, facing that fact and seeing the way I purposely distanced myself from other people were the beginning of a real change.

CHAPTER TWENTY-ONE

BUT I'M IN CONTROL
OF THE FORK

1990

Jean Nidetch moved to Las Vegas in 1990. A friend of hers, the television host Merv Griffin, sometimes filmed his show there, and he introduced Jean to the city. She gambled every day. It appears Jean traded one compulsion, eating, for another, gambling. Whatever the state of her dwindling finances, she was living, by her high standards, a simple life: she had a house with a pool—"But then, everybody in Las Vegas has a pool"—and a woman who came to clean once a week rather than a live-in housekeeper.

Her social circle included Claudine Williams, a major figure in the Nevada gambling industry as well as the first woman to manage a major Las Vegas Strip casino, and philanthropist Kitty Rodman. They were all donors to University of Nevada–Las Vegas. In 1993 Jean donated $1 million to the university to build a women's center, which is named for her, but little else remains in terms of a physical legacy or archives—the center doesn't even have any information about Jean's life on its own website. She gave additional money for scholarships for women who had grown up, like her, without money or who had otherwise overcome adversity. For this, the university gave Jean an honorary doctorate. After that FFH suffix she gave herself back in the 1960s, she finally became Dr. Nidetch and even had the honorific included on her business cards. Every year from the mid-1990s on, there would be a banquet for scholarship recipients and she'd give a speech. She'd tell her story, but it took on a slightly more universal and political tone. "I stood up for what I believed in as a woman. And I reached my goals regardless of what anyone says." She would gaze out at all the young women in the crowd and feel like she had done something tangibly good and lasting for her legacy. "I don't ask for anything," she told her recipients. "Except for you to keep in touch and tell me what you're doing." One woman who applied for a scholarship, Raquel O'Neill, didn't know who Jean was or why she had funded the program. Her application described being blind and reading braille. When she won, she met Jean, who told her she wanted to learn to read braille, and they became pen pals.

The Weight Watchers corporation had been doing well since people stopped using diet drugs to lose weight and once again returned to the fold of more traditional food-management diet programs. The success of the SmartPoints program and Sarah Ferguson's marketing campaign helped too.

The British newspaper *The Guardian* unearthed a confidential memo from an archive at the University of San Francisco written by an executive at the tobacco company Philip Morris in the late 1990s. Titled "Lessons Learned from the Tobacco Wars," it advised Kraft Foods (which had no ties to Weight Watchers, though Kraft would merge with Heinz in 2015) on strategies to deal with criticism of the company's role in the obesity epidemic. "The memo explains that just as consumers now blame cigarette companies for lung cancer, so they will end up blaming food companies for obesity, unless a panoply of defensive strategies are put into action."

Perhaps the magnitude of the obesity epidemic as well as ongoing efforts to stay profitable were what the Heinz corporation had in mind when William R. Johnson, Heinz's new president and CEO as of 1998, decided, after years of owning a diverse portfolio, to sell Weight Watchers. Or maybe it was just because Weight Watchers was faltering. Annual North American company–owned Weight Watchers meeting attendance dropped in 1997 to 7.8 million from 12.9 million in 1990, and in a filing to the Securities and Exchange Commission, Weight Watchers blamed the drop on Heinz's focus on selling prepackaged food. "These changes forced our group leaders to become food sales people and retail managers for food products, detracting from their function as role models and motivators for our members." For their part, Heinz executives said they wanted to refocus on the core business of food manufacturing. In 1999, Heinz sold Weight Watchers for $735 million in a leveraged buyout to Artal, an investment firm. The company had annual revenues of $365 million and profits of $47 million.

Linda Huett was a Yale Drama School–educated actress

who lived in London with a British husband and joined Weight Watchers after her twins' first birthday. She became a London-based Weight Watchers leader, then a manager, then vice president, and in 2000 she was named Weight Watchers International's CEO. Artal took the company public in 2001. (And incidentally, the terrorist attacks of September 11 actually boosted Weight Watchers' sales, as people tried to find healthy ways to cope with stress.) After Huett retired, David Kirchhoff, who had been the sixth employee of Weightwatchers.com, then a separate licensee of Weight Watchers, became the company's president and CEO in 2006. He wrote about his experience of losing forty pounds—which took him almost ten years—in a male-oriented weight-loss and business book called *Weight Loss Boss*, which came out in 2012.

Men were always about 10 percent of the Weight Watchers program and the advent of an internet-based plan that didn't force you to publicly weigh in or attend meetings suited their demographic. The company launched an online program specifically for men (seemingly for straight men, given the "manly" language used: "Lose like a man" and "Real men don't diet"). The Basketball Hall of Fame player Charles Barkley was the celebrity spokesman. The message was about sticking to the program and losing weight; it lacked the therapeutic tone of redemption often used on women and also the self-abnegation of how much this was all your fault.

The voice of the company began to shift away from goal weights as defined by a chart to focusing on smaller steps that might be more sustainable. In his book, Kirchhoff advocated losing 10 percent of one's body weight, which reduces the likelihood of type 2 diabetes by more than 50 percent, lowers systolic blood pressure, and can increase life expectancy by two to seven months. For the average woman who joined Weight Watchers, who was five four and 199 pounds, he wrote, "If we can shift our focus and simply concentrate on achieving a more realistic reduction in a sustainable way, we can win this fight collectively and as individuals." Program literature from the early 2000s states that "experts recommend that your initial goal be 10% of your present weight, an amount that makes a big difference in how you look and feel."

A feature story in *Elle* magazine on the newfound coolness of Weight Watchers published in the early 2000s read, "Perhaps you haven't heard, but Weight Watchers is *the* new power diet for fashionistas in L.A., not to mention Manhattan, Chicago, and San Francisco...In fact...Weight Watchers is suddenly so hot, one *Sex and the City* writer recently declared to her weekly meeting that doing it is better than winning an Emmy." *Sex and the City* did in fact include a Weight Watchers plotline for the character of Miranda as she tries to lose baby weight. She even finds a fellow Weight Watching hunk to date.

What to do with this newfound cool was another story. When the company got a call from Katie Couric saying she wanted to do Weight Watchers but was unable to attend meetings (or unwilling to be seen at one), CEO Kirchhoff called up Liz Josefsberg, a former Broadway actress who had lost sixty-five pounds on the plan and was working for Weight Watchers. He said, "I want you to create a black-ops program of Weight Watchers for Katie Couric, and any other celebrities to go along with." Personally coaching celebrities became Josefsberg's job. It was hands-on. They would call her from restaurants and she could tell them what to order. Jennifer Hudson had given birth the year before and wanted to play Winnie Mandela in a movie but was told she was too heavy, so she came to Weight Watchers too. Josefsberg was assigned to her and would fly out to Chicago, where Hudson lived, every week. "In the beginning, she was really struggling against it, trying to go really low on points and then overeating in other places," Josefsberg said. "But eventually she stuck to it." She'd tell Josefsberg, "If all I have to do is count points to look like this, wouldn't you?"

In October 2006, Jean's younger son, Richard, an actor who lived on the top floor of her house in Las Vegas, was moaning in pain. She called 911 and an ambulance took him to the hospital. "They said he had a tumor that burst, whatever that means," she wrote in her autobiography. He died in the hospital at age forty-nine. When Jean heard the news, she went deaf, as she had when she'd lost her first child. "He lived with me. We talked every night. I will never get over it. My first thought was to damage myself and I thought about it. But although I am not religious I do believe that if you commit suicide you won't go to heaven. I remember reading that somewhere. But when I get there I have to ask God—how come a parent should lose a child? It's like losing a limb, only worse," she said. Although it was never confirmed by the family, there were people close to the Nidetches who believed that Richard was a longtime addict and died of an overdose.

After Richard's death, Jean couldn't bear to live in Las Vegas and moved to Parkland, Florida, to be closer to the only family she had left—her son David. In Aston Gardens, a retirement community, she settled into a life of familiar rhythms. She ordered an omelet every morning and liked to sit at the table for singles, hoping she might meet someone interesting. Her friends knew that she would answer the telephone only between eleven a.m. and eleven p.m., no earlier and no later. Every Saturday she had her hair done, and she played poker five days a week. She would eat just one spoonful of ice cream every so often, converted to regular soda after her doctor told her to lay off artificial sweeteners, and often drank a nip of Baileys Irish Cream in the afternoon. ("You can't get drunk on Baileys. It just makes you sleepy!") She wore glittery blouses and giant green cocktail rings that she'd cheerily tell anyone were fake.

She didn't live in poverty in Florida by any means, but her apartment was small and spare. The walls of her living room were covered in photos from her glory days: people carrying BE LEAN WITH JEAN and JEAN THE QUEEN signs; Jean on the front page of a Las Vegas newspaper; Jean addressing the crowd at Madison Square Garden in 1973; Jean with her old flame Fred Astaire. "That is all I need. You can always buy clothes, you can always buy furniture. But you cannot replace pictures. To me they are the most memorable thing I own," she said. A small desk in the living room held her old Rolodex and a pile of unopened mail, some cards from Weight Watchers franchise holders. She owned forty-one albums of memorabilia that cluttered up the apartment, and she would whip them out if a visitor showed the slightest interest. The kitchen, however, was practically empty save for a few cans of soup. "I might regret not saving more, but this was never about the money," she said, often claiming in her later years not to have any idea how much she had in the bank. "It was about helping people, and their adoration is worth more than the money. I tell them, 'I know I could weigh 214 pounds again. I know it's possible. But I'm in control of the fork.'"

She still had the power to draw a crowd. When Jean made an appearance at a convention of Weight Watchers leaders in Orlando, CEO David Kirchhoff watched as women rushed the stage and angled to take photos, the same electric feeling as a Rolling Stones concert. "The whole place just completely erupted," he said. She had charisma, but more than that, she really believed in the power of weight loss to change lives. Members responded to her conviction. Sometimes in her retirement home, someone would whisper, "That's her," when she walked by in the hallway. She stayed camera-ready, keeping her hair bleached and set, conscious of her weight and appearance, as if she could be called on to be the Jean Nidetch whose face was on boxes of frozen food at any time. The thrill of attention was her deepest desire and motivator. Her longtime friend Florine Mark said, "She lived for recognition. For me the recognition I get from my family is the recognition. She had to find it from other people on the street or the press. She was kind of left alone."

There was a sadness to her. She told one reporter who interviewed her when she was eighty-four, "I know this is the finale of my life." By then she suffered from trigeminal neuralgia, which is a nerve inflammation that causes facial pain, and was slightly stooped and needed a walker to get around. Her short-term memory wasn't great. She had good days and bad days, and some who visited her suspected she might have dementia. Sometimes she would refuse to see visitors at all.

Jean Nidetch died on April 29, 2015, in her apartment in Parkland, at the age of ninety-one.

In her final years Jean increasingly felt like she had been forgotten by the company she had started. More than once she would call Weight Watchers headquarters in New York in the company of friends who were too polite or too sad to tell her to stop. Jean rang the head office in New York in front of one reporter, who dutifully chronicled the exchange:

Jean asked the unsuspecting woman on the switchboard, "Who invented Weight Watchers?"

"Oh my God! You don't know?" said the woman. "It was Jean Nidetch!"

"And is Jean Nidetch still alive?" asked the real Jean Nidetch, a tad mischievously.

"Oh my God! I hope so!" the receptionist replied. "Don't tell me she died!"

CHAPTER TWENTY-TWO

THIS TASTES SAD

May 2018

One rainy morning in May, Jennifer sent me a text. Don't judge me, **she wrote**. But I am participating in not one but two Weight Watchers challenges online. **Our Weight Watchers rapport had lately consisted of her texting me screenshots of posts from outlandishly committed people, like a woman with five children who got up daily at four a.m. to exercise to maintain her seventy-five-pound weight loss. I had no idea Jennifer was taking the endeavor so seriously.**

I'm listening, **I wrote back. She'd decided to join a group on-line that was doing a thirty-day plank challenge, where you held a plank pose for a whole minute every day for thirty days. And then once a week she did a zero-point day, mostly eating poultry or seafood and fruit and vegetables and legumes.** I'm so corny, **Jennifer wrote**. What's next? Am I going to become the kind of person who says "Sunday Funday"? Will I decorate my house with prints that read "Live, Laugh, Love" in script?

Am I going to have to pretend I never knew you? **I asked.**

I'd been trying to be a better, more emotionally available friend. First I took Vera out to dinner to talk about her life and her problems and I said we didn't have to talk about my body once the whole time, which was like passing our friendship's own version of the Bechdel test. We did, of course, but mostly to tease me about how I am now "so fitness" and "a late-in-life jock," two descriptions I would never have thought would apply to me.

For Jennifer's birthday in late May, I invited her over to celebrate and made, as an elaborate joke, a vintage Weight Watchers recipe. The one I chose was from the 1970s and called Crown Roast of Frankfurters. It was almost two dozen hot dogs cooked and then pinned together standing up in a circle to form an extremely crude approximation of an actual crown roast. I dumped some sauerkraut in the middle— the original recipe looked like it held washed coleslaw—and garnished it generously with sprigs of parsley and curlicues of mustard. I chose it because it didn't involve aspic or gelatin, unlike many recipes in the book (molded asparagus salad, chicken in aspic, lamb in aspic), and I actually love hot dogs and sauerkraut and mustard. At least, when served on a toasted bun on a hot summer night. "This tastes sad," Jennifer said after eating one bite. I shared with her a theory I had been working on that was heavily influenced by almost a year of browsing vintage Weight Watchers recipes. "Sometimes I think everyone was thinner in the sixties and seventies because the food was so gross." We ordered takeout from the Greek place near me and fed a large portion of the faux crown roast to my dog, Joan, who enjoys any and all food equally, from a decaying pizza crust she finds on the street to the leftover juice from cans of tuna.

"I know you were saying that no one seems to notice you lost weight, but I can," Jennifer said. I could feel myself blushing. Our relationship has always had a blithe, joking quality that runs on references to *Beverly Hills, 90210* and our shared love of celebrity memoirs. We have a lot of fun together but our feelings, more often than not, are unspoken. "You look good too," I told her. I didn't know how much Jennifer had lost, but I'd noticed her neck looked thinner—I hate to admit I'm that kind of appraising friend. We sounded like doddering fathers in sitcoms trying to express love. It's almost pathetic that we had a hard time even saying this to each other with twenty years of friendship already behind us. This is a woman who has seen me fall over on a treadmill while trying to wave at a guy I liked. I have peed in front of her on countless occasions. We have traveled to three continents together. But weight still manages to be something so complicated for both of us that we have to couch the subject in jokes and eye rolls and pretend like we know better than to care. But I can say we're slowly opening up about it.

I wonder what counts as progress. If our language around dieting has changed, I'm not sure our relationships with our bodies have. One problem that I—and a lot of people— have is knowing how to handle a society where an increasing emphasis is put on the individual, on the exception, the carve-out, the workaround, the personal triumph. Our culture veers wildly between impossible standards of beauty and seemingly impossible standards of acceptance, to terrible effect for almost everyone. Is weight not just another version of the tiresome conversation about whether women can have it all? Weight is part of a larger set of constraints with which women are forced to work and live and justify their humanity. And until we understand that those constraints are compulsory and that no decision about weight is entirely subjective, we as a society cannot fully comprehend the difficulty of being and only ever being seen as a fat woman.

I wouldn't wish the pain and shame I have felt since childhood around food and my body on anyone. I regret the money and effort I've spent on dieting. I wish I could restore what I have taken from myself. But at the same time, I don't fully accept body positivity, which presumes one is living in a vacuum and also doesn't acknowledge the reality of living in a fat body. Just the fact that I want to have the life I want and am willing to do what I must to get that life—that is an aspect of what motivates the dieter that gets lost when we talk about body acceptance. Am I part of the fat-positivity movement? My challenge is whether fat positivity has included me. One thing that frustrates me about body positivity is that the message is to do less. Stop dieting! Exercise when your body wants it! The hard truth is that we may be able to change our bodies faster than we can change society. Body acceptance says that it's my fault that I don't feel great about my body because I haven't fully committed to loving it. It's just a painted layer of positivity over the unresolved culture of dieting.

But diets only work if you stay on them forever, and who can do that? Who wants to do that? In his book on the history of dieting, *Never Satisfied*, Hillel Schwartz wrote that the wish to get slimmer "is the modern expression of an industrial society confused by its own desires and therefore never satisfied. On the one hand we seem to want more of everything; on the other hand we are suspicious of surplus...The culture of slimming has gradually asserted the primacy of flavor over substance. It has put into question our very sense of what is and what is not a food, what is an imitation and what is real." His solution was a kind of fat utopia where fat women "would not live in the future conditional, suspended between what they are and who they will be when they are finally thin. Fat women would not have to invent fantasy selves a quarter their bulk and four times as lovely."

Were this fat utopia open now and taking new residents, I'm not sure I'd be among them. For my whole life I have felt like I have been forced—or have forced myself—to choose between two opposing ideologies: to diet or to embrace not dieting. So much of my frustration stems from feeling like I have to choose one path or the other, working to change myself or hating myself, and I am destined to fail at both. Both paths represent an attempt to change myself *and* a reason to hate myself. The promises made on both sides are highly seductive. Do you find liberation through refusal or through acquiescence? My utopia is to reject both paths or, rather, to draw them together.

We are all trying to improve our lives, and no decision we make is binding. That's a false binary. Perhaps the only way forward is to understand that many of us might always want to diet and that we may in fact be happier and, possibly, healthier losing some weight. Dieting—whether or not you lose—can be addicting; restriction offers its own special kind of logic. Arriving at a nonbinary place takes work. It means you have to stop and think, a lot, about what you want, what society wants, and what you're willing to sacrifice. People love to ask, "What is the best diet?" The answer is the one that you can live with and not simply endure, the healthiest way of life that also keeps you happy. It's up to the individual to do the calculus of what that looks like. Peace is not blind capitulation to dieting culture or fat-acceptance culture.

We can want to lose weight for all kinds of reasons, from vanity to health. But at the same time we can want to live in a world where there's less importance put on what our bodies look like. I am just beginning to understand that I will always live in that paradox, that I accept myself as a person who struggles to change. If I can find greater happiness doing that with what I choose to eat and how much I weigh, imagine what I could do when applying it to the rest of my life.

At the meeting it was pouring rain outside and everyone was half complaining, half joking that being wet was messing with their weekly weigh-ins. Patrice had just returned from vacation in Barcelona. "I only gained three pounds," she said as the meeting began. "I told myself before I left, 'Patrice, you're going to gain weight, but no more than three pounds.' The food was so rich that I didn't need to eat a lot, so it was all from wine." Miriam mentioned that Weight Watchers sold proportioned wineglasses. They looked like regular wineglasses but had little etched lines indicating five ounces, six ounces, eight ounces. I heard Sadie, who was sitting in front of me, mutter, "Oh, please, it's not like you're going to bring that to a restaurant." She looked back and I whispered, "Or pack it in your suitcase and take it to a foreign country," and we both laughed.

The meeting's theme was "Boost Your Body Image." The weekly pamphlet featured an interview with a woman named Brittany from Wisconsin who referred to her stretch marks as "tiger stripes." I automatically hated her and closed it. Patrice said she had something to say about boosting her body image. "Six months after I had my son, all those years ago, I was sitting on the end of my bed and we were getting ready for a Christmas gathering. I went through everything in my closet, and none of it fit. It was bad. So I wore a huge red sweater and a black pair of tights," she said and laughed a little ruefully at the memory. She kept closing her eyes, like she was revisiting the scene of a crime while talking. "At the time I was eating pizza, burgers, not a lot of vegetables. I thought a salad was a bowl of croutons with cheese covered in ranch dressing. And now I've been doing this for two years and that picture still keeps me motivated. I really feel like I've become the woman I've always wanted to be." Miriam came over and gave her a hug. Everyone was nodding. There was not a person in that meeting who didn't have her own version of being forced to go to a party in a sweater and tights— even Jean never forgot the time she had to wear drapes to a costume party.

The big news was that Rosemarie had made her goal weight—155 pounds—and she gave a little victory speech. "I'm officially in the application process for the air force now. The recruiter told me if I could lose eighty pounds, I had the kind of character and discipline he was looking for," she said. We all clapped and cheered. I knew the air force would never want me—I don't even know how to drive a car—but in that moment I could see how accomplished and excited Rosemarie was. All forty of us in the room could relate when she talked about the specifics of her body, and maybe that was why we came again and again. "I can cross my legs. I can sit on my knees on the couch like a child. There are little things you never realize, like my girlfriend pointed out that I used to have to pick my foot up to tie my shoes and now I bend over," she said. "I bought a romper and a sleeveless shirt, clothes that I admired but never let myself buy before when I was a size eighteen. Now I'm a ten or an eight. My feet shrank a size!" I told her I had no idea your feet could shrink a whole size. "My hands too," she said. "I used to wear a large in gloves at work and now I wear a small."

I was so proud of her I wanted to give her a hug, but she was not very touchy-feely and we'd barely spoken. I was happy for her achievement and, frankly, jealous that she didn't share my ambivalence about the whole undertaking of dieting. She'd used Weight Watchers to totally transform her life, as had so many of the regulars I saw all the time. They had devoted themselves to these meetings and this diet to be the thing that did it. And I had not. That's why I felt different, even distant, from them.

I'd been pleased to find that Weight Watchers meetings weren't places of self-hatred. None of the members seemed like they had unrealistic goals or barely hidden eating disorders. It was a lot of discussion of tips and tricks and jokes and real support. I had become a member, if reluctantly, of a community. I could walk into a Weight Watchers at a strip mall in Michigan or in a church basement in England and feel some kind of home, even if it was not where I was going to meet my next best friends or how I was going to orient my life. I'd been reluctant to join Weight Watchers because it felt like the lowest common denominator. But maybe it's an equalizer. It's no-nonsense. In meetings and online, you are forced to hear from people outside of your daily bubble. It made me realize I wasn't all that special, which was in itself a huge relief.

When it comes to transformation, I know there is no shortcut for anyone, not for Rosemarie or for the women at the Body Love Conference. I said this to myself on days that I went to yoga and ate oatmeal and meditated and on days when I stopped tracking after a single meal totaled sixty-six points. When my dad and I had dinner at an Italian restaurant and he told me I didn't need to touch the bread basket. When my mom got her thyroid successfully removed, remarked that it looked like a piece of fried chicken, and then pointed out she hadn't eaten fried chicken in decades. When a friend sent a photo of me taken from the vantage point of a drone and my face looked like it was melting, with jowls pooling. I'd been Weight Watching so long, it sometimes felt like second nature and sometimes felt like I had lost all momentum. I had good days and I had bad days. Losing weight could fill me with optimism that the program was working, but it also, at times, scared me. Every pound lost came with a whole host of problems. When would I start liking the way I looked? How many more pounds until dating got easier? What if I gained it back yet again? Every retreat in the form of gaining a little weight back was met with disappointment but sometimes also felt like a slide back into comfort, the familiar, and the unthreatening.

CHAPTER TWENTY-THREE

LOSING WEIGHT CAN BE MAGIC

Weight loss can change your whole character. That always amazed me: Shedding
pounds does change your personality. It
changes your philosophy of life because
you recognize that you are capable of using
your mind to change your body.

—Jean Nidetch

Losing weight for Jean was magic; it symbolized potential,
and it had the potential to bring strangers together. "In
Israel, the Jews and Arabs sit together at our classes," Jean
Nidetch said to an Australian newspaper in 1993, "and, you
know, they don't hate each other at all. They're just interested in what they ate for breakfast." Jean believed that
sharing made us human and that struggling with weight
could be unifying rather than isolating. Out of frustration,
one could find community. Every one of us has our own
Frankenstein, our most-obsessed-over food, as Jean was so

fond of saying; we all have our particular version of cookies hidden in the bathroom hamper. And that was also her genius—if we all have complicated relationships with food, then we are all potential Weight Watchers members. She knew that what fat people needed more than a plan and a program was the support of each other, a place to vent or share notes or just listen. For Jean, a diet wasn't a tool of oppression but another way of keeping ourselves on track and having a plan for the future.

Jean had a Cinderella story for the ages. She was a maven and mogul who lost weight, spectacularly found her calling, and helped to create a national pastime and obsession that endures today. She may have been uneducated in the traditional sense but she was emotionally intelligent, charismatic, and understood instinctively how people's psychology worked. She had that elusive but clearly defined quality of authenticity.

Jean said, "You measure success by the length of time people can keep their lost pounds off." That's certainly how she measured her own success. But that strict definition was its own kind of prison. Jean lost a tremendous amount of weight and essentially, for the rest of her life, lived in the gilded cage of her own weight loss. She lived to keep it off, and establishing a business helped her do this, because it was a built-in narrative, but she wasn't able to be totally honest about the struggles attached to maintaining it. Not to her public, and maybe not even to herself. She swore that her original weight loss in the early 1960s was the full story, but reality was more complicated. The same could be said of her marriage, of her relationship with her children and with the

Lipperts, all of which she sacrificed to her ambition. Late in her life, she admitted she chose her career and company over her husband. "If I couldn't do it and stay married, I wouldn't stay married," she said. "I'm sorry about that and I suppose some people may judge me harshly for it, but it was also about believing in myself and trusting my instincts about where my life was taking me."

Jean's gamble didn't entirely pay off. When she stepped down from being president of Weight Watchers, she was stripped of her sense of self as an entrepreneur and businesswoman and she spent the full second half of her life listless and floundering. Jean was a fabulous woman who never actually had a real life as fabulous as she made it look on the outside. There is no one universal truth about who she was—an extrovert who craved a lot of validation from the outside world or a woman who didn't get enough credit for her achievements.

Jean was a stone-cold pioneer in whose footsteps a great many successful lifestyle and wellness entrepreneurs followed and made billions of dollars, for better and for worse. The problem for Jean with being a pioneer was that her fame was so new and original that the powers that be at the time didn't seem to quite know what to do with her. She certainly had cookbooks and frozen food and clothing patterns with her face on them, but if she were famous now, that would be just the beginning of an empire along the lines of Martha Stewart's or Ina Garten's or Gwyneth Paltrow's or Richard Simmons's or Sheryl Sandberg's. Jean was like the apotheosis of an influencer who used her own personal experience and her desire to evangelize from that experience as the cornerstone of her burgeoning empire. I enjoy Jean's cultural and corporate heirs, whom I'm pleased to see succeed, but it's hard to argue that the lure of perfection doesn't play an inextricable role in the mega-success of their aspirational businesses. She would have been a wonderful talk-show host. She might have been better remembered if she had named the company for herself, but she chose not to. She named it for its big idea.

Jean created modern dieting and in the process opened a Pandora's box. Dieting will never become obsolete but the way we talk about it has certainly changed. And the sensibility that Jean advocated isn't terribly sexy, nor is it in fashion in this era of food extremes.

The biggest lesson Jean taught me was one I don't think she would have wanted to share. She was a woman of appetite. She replaced that appetite for food with refusal. She used to tell journalists with great pride that she was never tempted by the potatoes served with her breakfast omelets and, in fact, had avoided them for decades. She liked to recount seeing an elegant lady at a party toying with her dessert, a parfait she would mix up while she was talking but never tasted. Jean thought showy acts of willpower like that were brilliant. Appetite is tricky; it finds ways to express itself elsewhere. When Jean could no longer get her thrills from food or being the public face of Weight Watchers, she channeled her energy into real estate, mink coats, poker games, major donations to charity, much of it beyond her means. She so craved love and attention—and was probably literally hungry for some cake or hash browns—that she lived lavishly to replace what she didn't have. Jean burned through the not insignificant $7 million she got from the Heinz sale. Hers is a cautionary tale. When we diet, what do we think we're giving up, and how are we compensating for it? Jean wanted a big life but what she got was a small one, dying alone and in denial. I'm not sure how happy she was with how it all turned out.

And yes, Jean is a footnote at Weight Watchers. In their New York City headquarters, etched into the ground in front of the reception area, is IT'S CHOICE, NOT CHANCE, THAT DETERMINES YOUR DESTINY—JEAN NIDETCH.

CHAPTER TWENTY-FOUR

THAT'S PROGRESS FOR ME

June 2018

We all need Jean.

She was a touch point for me. I applaud her tenacious desire to change herself, her conviction, her chutzpah—her drive to live a life that was a departure from the status quo. But I don't blindly agree with all Jean espoused. Her brand of dieting is a sometimes out-of-date model for self-transformation that manages to be painfully boring while also requiring a Herculean amount of willpower. If someone I knew brought a scale to a dinner party, I would probably suggest an intervention of some sort. I also refuse to villainize fatness the way Jean did, nor do I see it as an indication of laziness or lack of commitment. Coming to know her over this year has unlocked a new understanding of myself. She was a person from whose example I could come to know my own life better.

I don't think anyone would build a weight-loss campaign

around me. I didn't lose so much it solved all or any of my problems. I didn't magically transform into a thin person or a person who no longer craves sweets, nor did I become some kind of vixen who is irresistible to men. I am smart enough to admit that I don't even know if I'll be able to keep the weight I did lose off. The storyteller in me wanted to have a more dramatic conclusion to this story. I joked to people that I didn't expect to end it sixty pounds thinner and with a new fiancé in tow. But I wouldn't have minded that.

This is not a story of failure. To look "beyond the scale" (a Weight Watchers phrase that makes me cringe), I am healthier, my clothes fit better, I have fully committed to exercise. A Canadian friend sent me a bag of coveted ketchup-flavored potato chips from Toronto and they're still on my counter, unopened. I'll open them up when the time is right, probably with a group of friends. That's progress for me.

Maybe there isn't an ugly-duckling-turned-swan moment, no princess at the ball, no staircase to descend in front of one's prom date, no big reveal. I have been thinking about how much goes into changing your mind, yourself, and the world around you. There are the million decisions that must be made to maintain weight-loss momentum; the culture of abstemiousness that I resist for its boredom as much as anything else; and the inner conflict that weight loss amplifies. All of us are conflicted about our lives, our choices, the direction in which we are heading, what our lives have or haven't amounted to. And yet weight loss takes that large unruly conversation and imposes on it a strict narrative. There is incredible stress and pressure attached to having that narrative imposed on you and fear and uncertainty about living up to it. It's like a personal, physical, and emotional stress test. The desire to change myself is internal and personal but also social and universal, a response to a message that society (in a million forms) sends me and all of us.

Tomorrow will have a diet in it, maybe not a go-for-broke diet or even one that involves tracking calories, but I will always be conscious of what I eat and how much I exercise. That's why body neutrality doesn't feel like a good fit: I'm never going to stop wanting to be thinner or to stop chasing it. I know my life will always be this way, and I'm okay with that. That acceptance, even if it's an uneasy one, is my new normal.

How does a person know when to stop? Or to stop trying? I haven't stopped seeking the feeling of control that dieting gives me, but I have abandoned the narrative arc that being on a diet puts on our lives. Fat people are so often said to be living in the future, waiting for their thin physical selves to be revealed so their real lives can begin. I am not participating in that mind game. Unlike Jean, I don't consider changing myself a prerequisite for life to begin. I am focusing on the present, which means not lamenting all the times I have failed at dieting in the past and not focusing on some perfect future me that will suddenly be fine with the fact that my thighs touch when I walk. I have replaced some of the constant white noise of worry about my body with simply existing.

My victory looks very different from Jean's. I found that the highs and lows of dieting have kept me from appreciating the peace that could be mine if I could just put dieting into perspective—to move it away from the center of my life, where it was first placed without my will as a child, and relocate it to just one area among other daily realities. This is a more cerebral and abstract victory than Jean's, but I hope more enduring. I cannot separate my weight from myself, just as I cannot think of it as the source of all my problems.

We should all be allowed to eat and exercise and live in our bodies however we want to. For me the relentlessness of body commentary weighed heavily. Being at Weight Watchers for a year showed me that some people don't agonize about the politics of this as much as I do, but the question of how much you're willing to change yourself to fit in applies to so many of us and even more so when you don't fit into the beauty ideal. I have had to accept that I might be able to change my fat body faster than this culture will change how it views, treats, and accommodates fat bodies. Losing weight wasn't going to make me happier—which may have been the bitterest part of all—but I also understand that pounds lost are not the only victory.

An essential truth about being a woman is that we have so many internalized messages that we are not enough that we might spend our whole lives coming to terms with them. And weight is sometimes the physical relic left behind from this struggle. I have been afforded the privilege to concentrate on this unfairness, but those ideas have seeped into other parts of my life as well. Who gets to move through the world with ease? It shouldn't just be those in the pinnacle of power, a white man of a certain socioeconomic status or a young woman who looks like a supermodel.

Dieting usually requires us to choose to live smaller lives—and by smaller, I don't mean in pants size, I mean in experience. Losing weight is a tithe you never quit paying.

It's relentless. You can sacrifice everything at the altar of the bitch goddess of weight loss and it ultimately won't be enough. That was certainly one of the more tragic lessons of Jean's life. Dieting forces a lack of spontaneity, a fear of the new, an unwillingness to deviate from the plan. It's so at odds with every other way I live my life. Because both dieting and body acceptance are unfulfilling, I prefer to look at the larger picture.

I am tempted to think I have wasted half my life obsessing over my weight. But I feel exhilarated about the rest of the life that I have ahead of me. To live big is to stand out. By facing the extent of my unhappiness and how much of that unhappiness was connected to my body, I got to know myself. I have come to understand my own hunger more, and it isn't to lose weight above all else. I will make my choices on my own terms. That goes for dieting or any other part of my life. I'm not going to do anything out of fear of the final weigh-in.

I didn't weigh in at my last meeting of my Weight Watchers year, just before my forty-first birthday. Initially I skipped the scale because I didn't get there early enough to weigh myself. I sat down just as Miriam announced that she had in fact had the best arms at her high-school reunion at Bronx Science, where her older daughter just graduated with honors. Miriam's hair was dyed ice blue and lavender and she was wearing the same black-and-white polka-dot shift dress as the first time I saw her. The meeting went on, some members first-timers, others veterans. Something Miriam said resonated with me. "What does it mean to you to take a weight-loss break?" Jean would probably roll over in her grave at such a relaxed view of dieting coming from the company she founded.

And so I left that meeting without even weighing myself. I know I lost around twenty pounds over the year. There will be more meetings in my future, maybe not every week, and sometimes I will choose to bypass the scale. Those twenty pounds don't seem like a life-changing number—they aren't, if you go by the "before" and "after" photos—but that's not how I will remember this year. My body was simply what changed the least.

ACKNOWLEDGMENTS

This book would not exist without my agent and friend Jen Marshall, who encouraged me to find Jean's voice—and my own. Thank you to David Kuhn and everyone at Aevitas Creative Management.

I was lucky to work with Vanessa Mobley, who pushed me to think deeper and more critically, and with Reagan Arthur and the whole team at Little, Brown.

I owe so much to Alexandra Jacobs and every editor who assigned a story that informed this book.

I am so grateful to everyone at WW International Inc. who sat for interviews, including Mindy Grossman and Gary Foster, and to the staff there who so gamely lent a hand in research: Stacie Sherer, Jenny Zimmerman, Brooke Theiss, Sara Bosco, Nimra Butt, and Paul Kalis.

Christina McCausland and Zara Golden were invaluable

in their research assistance. Rebecca Federman at the New York Public Library, Alison Kelly at the Library of Congress, Laura Shapiro, and Alexis Coe all generously gave their time and expertise. *Good Housekeeping* opened up its cookbook library to me.

Thanks to Rosalie Swedlin and Alex Goldstone for your enthusiasm.

I cherish my early readers Jami Attenberg and Lauren Mechling. Special thanks to Windy Chien, Whitney Joiner, Scandal Club, and my Sky Ting/Moves/Ballet1/Sacred Fig/ Love Yoga family for friendship, mental health, and always asking how the book was going.

And to my parents: Thank you, I love you.

ABOUT THE AUTHOR

Marisa Meltzer is a journalist based in New York who writes the Me Time column for the *New York Times* Style section and has contributed to *The New Yorker, The Guardian, Vanity Fair,* and *Vogue,* among numerous other major national publications. The author of two previous books, *How Sassy Changed My Life* and *Girl Power,* she lives in Brooklyn and was born in Northern California.